SCHIZOPHRENIA
SIMPLY UNDERSTOOD

Developing the Basis for
a Correct Understanding,
Healing, and Recovery
Model

Ty C. Colbert, Ph.D.

KEVCO PUBLISHING

ORANGE, CALIFORNIA

SCHIZOPHRENIA
SIMPLY UNDERSTOOD

*"A personality, a life history, a pattern of hopes
and desires lie behind the psychosis.
The fault is ours if we do not
understand them."*

Carl Jung, M.D.

*"Schizophrenia is the loss of dreams,
not the loss of dopamine"*

Dan Fisher, M.D., Ph.D.

THE EMOTIONAL PAIN DIAGRAM

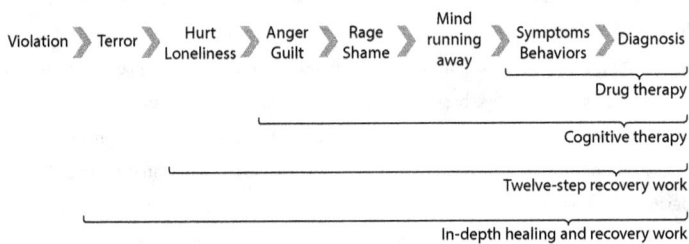

Violation ⟩ Terror ⟩ Hurt Loneliness ⟩ Anger Guilt ⟩ Rage Shame ⟩ Mind running away ⟩ Symptoms Behaviors ⟩ Diagnosis

Drug therapy

Cognitive therapy

Twelve-step recovery work

In-depth healing and recovery work

Colbert, Ty C.

Schizophrenia-simply understood: developing the basis for a correct understanding, healing, and recovery model/by Ty C. Colbert, Ph.D.

ISBN 978-0-9891607-4-2

1. Schizophrenia-Etiology. 2. Schizophrenia—Therapy. 3. Mental illness. 4. Mental health. 5. Psychotherapy. I. Title

Contents

Introduction

As a clinical psychologist, I have, for the last 35 years, had a personal interest in the study of what is referred to as "schizophrenia." As a result of this interest, in 2016 I published a 540-page book titled *Healing Runaway Minds* and a corresponding 200-page workbook titled *From Breakdown to Breakthrough*. Both publications place a special emphasis on the recovery possibilities of this so-called disorder. It was at this point that I felt I needed to write a smaller book with the goal of easily and concisely explaining this mysterious human condition.

When I use the terms *easily* and *concisely*, I don't mean to over-simplify this condition or to minimize the accompanying pain experienced by those suffering from it. As you may already know, or will soon learn, a massive amount of confusion surrounds this topic. Again, much of the confusion exists because of individuals and professionals also not having a clear understanding of the origin or cause of this condition. Consequently, my main goal with this book is to develop an understanding that simply *makes sense* to anyone reading this material. This, of course, will create the best path to take in order to help the suffering individual, and to give guidance to those who wish to help those who are suffering.

Before we start, I want to quickly address a couple of issues.

PSYCHIATRIC TERMS

As I have mentioned in my other books, and during my career as a clinical psychologist, I place very little emphasis on giving a person a specific psychiatric diagnosis. The reason is simple. As you will discover, especially with individuals diagnosed with schizophrenia, the number and types of symptoms exhibited by such individuals are almost unlimited. That is because, when the person's unconscious mind attempts to adjust to an overload of emotional pain, it will create whatever way is needed. At times the person may become extremely depressed for a while, then manic. Or, in more extreme cases, a person's unconscious may freeze parts of the person's body in a catatonic state or create fictitious voices.

The important point to this writer and many other professionals is not a particular diagnosis, but the understanding and eventual healing of the person's emotional pain that is at the root of the problem.

On the other hand, I will use certain common terms such as schizophrenia to best communicate what is needed. But, as you will see, when I use the term schizophrenia in particular, I am not referring to some disease, but to an emotionally hurting person.

EXAMPLES USED IN THIS BOOK

Several of the examples or case studies that I will use in this book have also been used in the other two books mentioned above. I am reusing these examples because of their teaching quality and because the identities of those individuals have been adequately disguised.

PART I

What Causes Humans to Act in "Weird" or "Hard-to-Understand" Ways?

IT IS STILL A GREAT MYSTERY, both within the professional community and among the general public, as to what causes the symptoms associated with and/or used to diagnose a person with schizophrenia. Is such behavior due to some biological defect, mainly bad genes or chemical imbalances? Or is the behavior the result of some out-of-control emotions and thoughts? After all, anyone is capable of acting in strange ways at times.

Asking this basic question reminds me of my first encounter with a so-called mad, highly disturbed, "schizophrenic" person. The year was 1971, and I had just started teaching at a high school in a city a few miles east of downtown Los Angeles.

As I drove down a main street to get to and from work, I often noticed a man standing on the sidewalk making no verbal sounds, but most likely having an intense argument with an imaginary person he believed was standing directly in front of him. This man would fling his arms around in a seemingly agitated manner, talking as fast as he could, but always with no actual sounds coming from his mouth. Since there was no one visibly standing directly in front of him, most likely he was hallucinating or arguing with a person that he was imagining was present.

He did not fling his arms around as if he was trying to hit someone, but was simply expressing himself in an extremely animated way. Furthermore, since he was there most days and to the best of my knowledge, he had not become aggressive toward others around him, those who saw him did not seem to be overly bothered by his behavior.

Just down the street from the high school was a coffee shop that I occasionally visited. This same man would also frequent this place, always sitting at the counter and ordering only a cup of coffee.

Here is what I found most interesting about his behavior. After ordering his coffee and settling in, if there was a vacant counter seat next to him, it wasn't long before he started having a conversation or argument with some imaginary person supposedly sitting in the vacant seat. He did not fling his arms around as much, but he still silently moved his lips as if energetically talking with someone. Again, because he made no verbal sounds and did not act aggressively inside the restaurant, and because the regulars were familiar with his behavior, no one paid any special attention to him.

But here is what got me to thinking about his behavior in particular and later schizophrenia in general. On the one hand, he seemed almost completely out of control or perhaps was compelled to act out. When he did, he would turn his head 90 degrees to directly face the empty seat or the imaginary person.

Yet, when the waitress, who was obviously quite familiar with his behavior, came up to ask him if he wanted more coffee, he would immediately snap out of his "psychotic" state and respond appropriately to her. "Yes, I would like some more coffee and some cream as well. Thank you."

He would also at times appear to be having a normal conversation with the waitress just as any other customer would. But when left alone for a short time, if the seat next to him was vacant, it wouldn't be long before some part of him would compel him to once more start up an emotionally-charged conversation with an imaginary person.

Even though I was certified to teach math in high school at the time, I had to take a couple of psychology classes in order to obtain my state teaching credential. In one of these classes I was taught that schizophrenia in particular was a biological disease due to perhaps defective genes and/or chemical imbalances. But if this were true, how and why was this individual able to so quickly snap out of his so-called mental illness-like behavior and act perfectly normal or sane for a short time, and then after a period of time, feel apparently compelled to have an argument or a highly charged discussion with someone who did not exist to the rest of us?

If there was some biologically defective element involved, how could he turn it on and off at will? In other words, how could he choose to act "normal" when necessary, but then "lose his sanity," so to speak? Something just did not make sense to me.

IS NOT SUCH BEHAVIOR CHARACTERISTIC OF HUMAN NATURE IN GENERAL?

Certainly one of the great mysteries concerning human behavior is how and why any of us can suddenly act in weird and unexplainable ways. For example, a father who has had a rough day at work may come home with little emotional energy left to handle any additional stressors. Then, after being home for a while, he may begin to act out in hard-to-understand ways. At this point, the rest of the family may look at each other as if to say, "What's going on with Dad? He sure is acting weird." The truth is that a mother, wife, boss, teacher, friend, lover, child, or any one of us for that matter, is capable of acting out in ways that just don't seem to make sense to themselves and others at the moment.

Most often, if a loving and understanding wife were to calmly ask her husband or child if he or she had a rough day, that person, because of the felt safety, may then be able to reflect upon his or her day and make sense out of the behavior. The husband might say, "Oh, I had some real tough and demanding customers to deal with today." Or the child might say, "Mommy, the kids are picking on me again for how I look."

With such an approach by the wife toward her husband especially, and the husband's ability to reflect upon his stressful day, an instant element of sanity most likely will result, and both the husband and wife will be able to emotionally relax.

Likewise, a child who was teased at school may come home with some unexpected, strange, and unexplainable behavior. But if the parent can take the time, with some felt love and acceptance, to calm the child's mind down, that parent may learn the true driving force behind the child's behavior.

BUT WHAT ABOUT THE BEHAVIOR OF THE SO-CALLED SCHIZOPHRENIC?

Thus, if we are willing to admit to it, any of us can act pretty weird at times, yet snap out of it when we need to or with some help. So, what about the behavior or symptoms used to diagnose or label someone with schizophrenia? Again, are these just more extreme appearing behaviors, or are they the result of some biological brain disease?

The truth is that biologically-orientated psychiatry has been obsessively and frantically hunting for some biological causal defect for nearly 100 years and absolutely nothing has been found. In reference to a possible chemical imbalance, neuroscientist Steven Hyman, past director of the National Institute of Mental Health, recently stated that psychotropic drugs are similar to drugs of abuse (street drugs), in that they work by disabling the brain.[1] In other words, they work by suppressing a person's emotions and thoughts.

More recently, Jan Olav Johannessen, chair of the 55-year-old international professional organization, The International Society for Psychological and Social Approaches to Psychosis, stated, "I think it is fair to state that the search for the Schizophrenic gene has failed."[2]

In an online article published in 2013, psychiatrist Philip Thomas, M.D., confirmed much the same. In reference to a genetic basis, he reported that after 50 years, research has revealed no evidence of a genetic basis for the condition.[3]

Thomas continued by quoting the work of Kendell and Jablensky. According to them, most contemporary psychiatric disorders, even those such as schizophrenia that have a pedigree stretching back to the nineteenth century, cannot yet be described as valid disease categories.

Thomas then summarized the overall recovery rates of several long-term studies. "In broad terms 50% or more of people with the diagnosis make a significant recovery."[4]

Actually, two research projects conducted by the World Health Organization (WHO) in 1969 and 1978 threw as much doubt into a biological model for schizophrenia as any set of studies. WHO investigated the results of the treatment of schizophrenia in developing countries such as India and Colombia and then compared these results with those in developed countries such as the United States, where more "advanced" psychiatric treatments were offered. Nearly two-thirds of the patients in the developing countries had positive outcomes, whereas only slightly over one-third had successful outcomes in the developed countries.[5]

According to Dr. Peter Breggin, these results showed that "patients diagnosed with schizophrenia actually do better in third world countries where they receive little or no drugs and are supported by an extended family."[6] Assen Jablensky, M.D., in his analysis of these studies, stated, "The strongest evidence at present is that of an environmental effect on course and outcome of schizophrenia."[7]

Robert Whitaker, author of *Mad In America*, later wrote,

> The WHO studies, however, did more than just challenge American psychiatry to rethink its devotion to neuroleptics [antipsychotics]. The studies challenged American psychiatry to rethink its whole conception of the disorder. The studies had proven that recovery from schizophrenia was not just possible, but common—at least in countries where patients were not continually kept on antipsychotic medications. The WHO studies had demonstrated that the American belief that schizophrenics necessarily suffered from a biological brain disorder, and thus needed to be on drugs for life, wasn't true.[8]

Quoting psychologist Paris Williams from his book *Rethinking Madness*,

> It is also of great interest to note that the use of antipsychotic drugs... is inversely correlated with good recovery outcomes.... The countries with the highest percentage of residents using antipsychotic drugs showed the worst recovery rates; and the countries with the lowest percentage of residents using antipsychotics showed the best recovery rates.[9]

These studies raised at least two important questions. First, if disorders such as schizophrenia are biological, why is the recovery rate higher with the least amount of psychiatric treatment? Second, if not biologically-based, is there something fundamentally wrong with the present-day biopsychiatric model?

BACK TO THE BIG QUESTION

So, I guess we are back to the start. What could cause the man on the sidewalk (or any of us) to act the way he did, to lose control over his behavior and emotions, but then under certain circumstances almost instantly regain control? To answer this question and to eventually help individuals diagnosed with schizophrenia, we must take some time to attempt to understand what makes human beings different from the rest of the animal world. Specifically, I am referring to human consciousness, or the ability to reflect upon ourselves, and also the corresponding ability of our unconscious to take charge and direct aspects of our lives.

To begin to understand the role that human consciousness can and often does play in the development of hard-to-understand behavior, let me present you with a few examples. I ran across the first example while collecting material for my dissertation, and it is one I also used in *Healing Runaway Minds*.

This example took place on the battlefields of World War II. The right hand of one of the soldiers on the front lines suddenly became paralyzed. It was frozen in an open gripping position, as if he were about to throw a baseball. As a result of his paralysis, he was brought back to a hospital for testing. After several neurological and medical tests were conducted, the doctors could not find anything physiologically wrong with his hand or his nervous system.

Then one day, while he was lying on his stomach on a bed, a nurse came by and noticed how uncomfortable he was with his hand frozen open. She offered to massage his back, to which he agreed. As she began the massage, she noticed a section of his back that seemed extremely tense, so she concentrated on that area. After a couple of minutes, the soldier suddenly broke down crying. He continued to weep uncontrollably for some time, but by the time he had stopped crying, his hand had relaxed and the paralysis was gone.

Shortly afterwards, certain memories began to emerge, until he had a full picture of the incident that had caused the paralysis. He had been on the front lines with his best army friend, looking for enemy troops. He and his friend had suddenly come across several enemy soldiers. They quickly hid behind a fallen tree, hoping not to reveal their location or that of their company. When the enemy began to walk their way, he pulled out a hand grenade. As he prepared to throw it, he realized that the explosion would expose their position, as well as the company's, so he chose not to throw it. A few minutes later, one of the approaching soldiers noticed them and opened fire. He got away, but his best friend was killed in the firefight.

Soon after making it back to safety, he began to think about what had just taken place. The fact that he might have saved his friend's life by throwing the hand grenade was too much for him to handle emotionally. So a protective part of his mind took over and blocked out everything, back to the moment just prior to making the decision not to throw the grenade. His mind was able to freeze time, but it also froze a part of his body as a result.

To explain this mysterious process a little better, let's go back to his moment of decision. The soldier had the grenade in his hand, which was cocked, ready to throw. At the same time, his back muscles were flexed to unload the grenade; or possibly his back simply tightened up due to the fear of having to make such a critical decision.

Then he chose not to throw the grenade and his friend was killed as a result. Perhaps because he may already have been emotionally overloaded from witnessing other killings or killing enemy troops himself, this event pushed him over the edge. He did not have enough emotional strength left to take on the possible responsibility of his friend's death, even though he had made what he considered the best choice at the time. Consequently, most of the feelings and memories associated with the event had to be blocked out.

As he returned to the safety of his company and as the feelings began to surface, his unconscious chose not to allow him to be aware of what had actually happened. His mind froze time for him in this particular area of his life. It worked so effectively that in doing so, it froze part of his body. In this way, it completely blocked out the incident. A combination of the warmth of the nurse's care and the safety of the hospital allowed his unconscious side to finally relax his mind and body, letting his feelings and memories rise to full consciousness.

Now let me ask you a question at this point. Do you see the similarities between this event and the examples of the father coming home from work or the child teased at school? First comes the trauma, then the suppression of that trauma. The suppression of the trauma eventually results in some hard-to-explain behavior. But upon the unconditional loving care, and the safety given by another person, the suffering person is able to *revisit* the trauma, resulting in an emotional healing. Finally, as a result of that healing, the "abnormal" behaviors are no longer *needed*.

Also note that a person is not necessarily required to have experienced a major trauma for such behavior to occur. It certainly was a major trauma with the soldier, but for the father and the child, the symptoms were the result of more everyday kinds of traumatic events. I bring up this point because, as you will see, the key to understanding the behavior of the "identified" schizophrenic person is to simply see the behavior as an exaggeration of anyone's stressed-out or traumatized behavior.

As unique as the above story of the soldier may seem, the same kind of unconscious process can happen to any of us. The following example comes from my own life. As I share it, you may find it worthwhile to attempt to identify an example or two from your own life.

I grew up as an extremely shy person. I was one of those kids who had a deadly fear of standing up in front of the class to give a presentation or even being called upon from my seat. In fact, I used to slouch down in order to hide behind the person in front of me if I suspected the teacher wanted to call on someone.

Today I have mastered this fear and, in fact, look forward to speaking in front of groups. But an unconscious "protective" part of my mind has learned how to help me out. One time after giving a talk to a large audience, it suddenly dawned on me that I had become completely blind to the audience during the talk. I had spent an hour looking at them but realized that I had not registered seeing one single face. In order to reduce my anxiety or fear of rejection, my mind or my unconscious had somehow cut off all visual awareness of the audience.

To clarify, I did not actually become physically blind because, after all, I could still read my notes. But an aspect of my unconsciousness somehow blocked out and/or prevented certain information from reaching conscious awareness, thus keeping my selfhood from full exposure to the situation.

On other occasions, after giving a talk and upon reflection, I have noticed that I had seen perhaps only one face with any degree of clarity; usually a smiling person who was bobbing her head up and down in agreement with me. So, as a protective measure, a part of my consciousness was choosing to either cut off all awareness or just see the face of the person in agreement.

But what about a person who has been officially diagnosed with schizophrenia? Again, if the behavior is examined closely enough, eventually the behavior is present as a result of the person's *emotional* condition, not due to some *physical* condition. Let's look at a couple of other examples.

In his biography, Dr. Dan Fisher shared that he grew up in the 1950s believing in science and the slogan, "Better living through chemistry." He eventually earned a Ph.D. in biochemistry and went to work for the National Institute of Mental Health (NIMH), attempting to discover the chemical causes of mental illnesses. At that time, he believed that disorders such as schizophrenia and depression were caused by a biochemical imbalance in the brain and that the best treatment was the administration of a drug.

Due to emotional issues, which included the failure of a close relationship, he was hospitalized at the age of 25 and diagnosed with schizophrenia. He had become so deeply involved with his work that he actually started to believe he was a neurotransmitter. He reported seeing a particular chemical (phenylalanine hydroxylase enzyme) shooting at him and having to add oxygen to it to avoid injury. As a result, he was hospitalized.

After being subjected to the standard psychiatric care that consisted primarily of medication, he eventually realized that

> ...this breakdown was a call to change some of my perceptions about myself and the way I was living. In order to recover I had to develop a new personal philosophy and deeper relationships. I also had to change my work to be more people-focused so that I could see the impact of my work firsthand.[10]

Dr. Fisher went back to school, eventually earning his M.D. degree and specializing in psychiatry. For the past 20-plus years, Dr. Fisher has worked as a board-certified psychiatrist, teaching others that recovery is possible. In 2002, he was appointed to the White House New Freedom Commission on Mental Health. Through his efforts and his obvious recovery, the committee established its major goal of transforming the mental health system from a maintenance or symptom-reduction system to a consumer-and-family-driven, recovery-oriented approach to care. In the words of the commission, "We envision a future when everyone with a mental illness will recover."[11]

Dr. Fisher and his organization, The National Empowerment Center, represent one model in a growing international recovery movement, all with much the same goals as established by this commission.

Here is another example that I will refer to later on.

A father once brought his psychotic 23-year-old son, Mark, to me for an evaluation. Mark had been living on the streets of Hollywood for several years and had prostituted himself as a way of supporting himself and his drug habit. Although he had been free of street drugs for several months, his previous drug use complicated the attempt to isolate the origin or reason for his psychotic symptoms.

As I talked with Mark, like the person in the local coffee shop that I spoke of earlier, he continued to switch from a state of coherency or "sanity" to an extremely delusional state, described by his extraordinary relationship with Jesus. He shared that at certain times, a glorious light beam would appear from the sky and envelop him. Within this beam, Jesus would then appear to purify him.

Initially, it appeared that his psychotic behavior came out of nowhere, perhaps as a result of brain damage from his use of street drugs. As I continued to listen to and observe Mark, paying close attention to his body language and the specifics of the conversation, I discovered a very precise link between his emotional pain and his psychotic behavior.

If I directed the conversation to topics void of any strong emotional content (foods, music, etc.), he remained relatively free of any psychotic symptoms. But the moment I approached certain areas of his painful life (e.g., "Was it hard to support yourself on the street?"), he immediately escaped into his religious and delusional monologue.

The intentional protectiveness of Mark's psychotic behavior was quite obvious to me. He felt an overload of shame and guilt from prostituting himself. So his mind simply dissociated at such times, believing during those moments that he was in the "light of Jesus" and thus this light was either keeping his soul or selfhood pure, or something to that effect. In other words, his unconscious mind had taken over in much the same way it had for the soldier and me, not due to some unknown disease, but as a *protective* mechanism.

A CONSISTENT PATTERN

Once again, do you recognize the consistent pattern with all these examples? Think back to the fictitious example of the father and the child, the soldier, Dan Fisher's trouble with a key relationship and some other issues, as well as mine and Mark's. Don't they all illustrate a similar pattern?

The following is one of my favorite "moments of truth" from the highly gifted psychiatrist Frieda Fromm-Reichmann. At the time she made the following observation, she was in London helping people adjust to the nightly bombing raids by Nazi Germany during WWII. This passage actually comes from the biography, *To Redeem One Person Is to Redeem the World,* by Gail Hornstein. During the sustained strategic bombing of Britain by Germany in WWII, some of Reichmann's colleagues noticed the extremely low incidence of psychiatric symptoms among civilian victims. Reflecting upon this situation, Hornstein stated,

> A few people had needed sedation for brief periods, but if they were brought to a mobile unit right after the bombing and encouraged to express their feelings, even these

victims had recovered "immediately and completely, no matter how severe the actual incident had been." Chronic disturbances occurred only among people unable to verbalize their terror.[12]

Continuing, the biographer stated,

Frieda argued that these findings precisely fit a psychoanalytic model of trauma. Millions of people faced violence and horror in their lives, yet few became psychotic. Therefore, it couldn't be the trauma itself that produced mental illness; it had to be the repression of the trauma—the cutting off of the event from subsequent experience....[13]

Following is a timeline depiction of the process I am describing:

Violating events	Mind suppresses	Person triggered	Hard-to-understand behavior/ thoughts	Mental Illness diagnosis given

And here is the corresponding healing and recovery process:

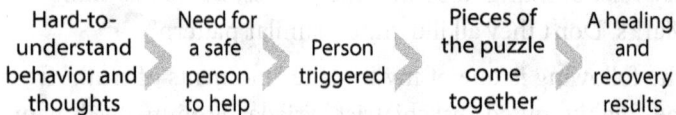

Hard-to-understand behavior and thoughts	Need for a safe person to help	Person triggered	Pieces of the puzzle come together	A healing and recovery results

Obviously, the process is usually much more difficult than explained above, but sometimes it isn't. Let me share another example that I also used in my book *Healing Runaway Minds*.

I once counseled a teenager who, while at her home, suddenly took off all her clothes and proceeded to run naked down the street. She was subsequently hospitalized and given a preliminary diagnosis of schizophrenia. She later believed she had acted this way because she remembered feeling a tremendous sense of freedom doing the same activity in her backyard when she was a young child. Thus, perhaps extremely stressed out in her life, her mind came up with a "creative" solution to keep her from completely crashing emotionally.

I personally believe that in most, if not all, similar situations, a psychotic break can be seen as an emotional "cry for help." The person, for whatever reason, has become so overloaded with emotional pain, and feels almost totally helpless to properly address that pain, that the pain suddenly surfaces. When it does, any kind of behavior is possible.

Thus, at the point of such a break, it may be much more important to *not* attempt to make immediate sense out of the behavior, but to simply realize that the person is hurting emotionally and is desperate for help.

A LITTLE MORE ON HUMAN CONSCIOUSNESS

You still may be asking the big question, "How can such a straightforward model explain all the more difficult-to-understand behaviors and thought patterns that can accompany a person diagnosed with schizophrenia?"

To answer this question, we need to take a closer look at what makes us unique; specifically, human consciousness. Even though Freud and many others before him struggled to develop an understanding of human consciousness and its corresponding ability to suppress awareness, the simple truth is that the nature of consciousness is not discussed much today within my profession.

"Why?" you may ask. The reason is a simple one. The scientific and/or medical professional community can't get a handle on this aspect of human nature to figure it out, including its origin, nature, exact function, location in the brain or body, and so forth. Even with all the advancement in brain imaging and genetic technology, scientists appear to know next to nothing about this aspect of human nature. Quoting Judi Chambers, author of *The Conscious Mind: In Search of a Fundamental Theory*,

Consciousness, however, is as perplexing as it ever was. It still seems utterly mysterious that the causation of behavior should be accompanied by a subjective inner life... We do not just lack a detailed theory; we are entirely in the dark about how consciousness fits into the natural order.[14]

The author then followed with this: "The easiest way to develop a theory of consciousness is to deny its existence...."[15]

The International Dictionary of Psychology struggles to define consciousness in much the same way, stating that, "Consciousness is a fascinating but elusive phenomenon: It is impossible to specify what it is, what it does, or why it evolved. Nothing worth reading has been written about it."[16]

For my doctorate in psychology, I chose a program based on an existential philosophy. One of my first courses was a basic theories course taught by Dr. William Ofman, who had written a key book on the subject titled *Affirmation and Reality*. From the very start, he put consciousness at the forefront of the attempt to understand certain aspects of human behavior.

In one of his earlier lectures, he mentioned that somewhere in the evolutionary process, consciousness, or the ability for a species such as human beings to introspect, suddenly evolved. (These may not have been his exact words, but it is what I remember from what he had said.)

As a Christian, I would naturally struggle with an evolutionary view of consciousness, but I had no problem accepting that somehow consciousness suddenly appeared. After all, the Bible gives an account of God choosing to breathe His spirit into us, thus giving us the ability to communicate with Him, ourselves, and others.

I mention this point not to attempt to bring religion into the conversation, but to help summarize our search for the origin and an eventual understanding of human consciousness. So, in summary, even with all of their advanced equipment, scientists know almost nothing about this semi-independent aspect of our lives. Thus for right now, all we can say for sure is that it suddenly appeared as either a product of the evolutionary process or as an act of God.

THE POWER OF OUR UNCONSCIOUSNESS, DISSOCIATING MIND

In the attempt to understand the almost unlimited forms of behavior, beliefs, and thoughts that can accompany a diagnosis of schizophrenia, we basically have two choices. Either we can believe that such behavior is the result of a defective brain, or it is the person's unconscious mind working to overpower the conscious self for some specific set of reasons.

If a diseased brain or defective system is believed, then recovery or healing is obviously dependent upon the correction of the defect(s). Thus, until a correction can be made, the suffering person is at the mercy of science and the use of drugs to suppress the undesirable symptoms.

But what if it is the person's unconscious mind that is "creating" those symptoms and behaviors due to past trauma (or series of small felt traumas, i.e. peer pressure)? If so, then there is hope today through a proper healing and recovery program. Since biological psychiatry and major research institutions such as the NIMH have admitted that no actual biological defects have been established, and there is an overwhelming amount of evidence that individuals can recover through personal growth and proper psychological care, we need to spend a little more time on the concept of human consciousness and the corresponding unconscious.

Once more, the scientific community knows very little about the origin, location, and substance of consciousness. But we do know of its power through our own personal experiences and those of others. I have already mentioned a couple of examples, the soldier with the crippled hand and my blindness when speaking, but let me share some additional information along these same lines by starting with the topic of hypnosis.

The beginning of modern psychodynamic thinking, as well as the discovery of the unconscious, came about as a result of a growing understanding and application of hypnosis. At the beginning of the exploration of this topic, Friedrich Anton Mesmer (1733–1815) was able to treat individuals who appeared to be suffering from a physical disability (e.g., deafness or paralysis) for which no organic cause could be found.

Many years later, two other physicians, Ambrose Auguste Liébault (1823–1904) and Hippolyte-Marie Bernheim (1840–1919), began to work together using hypnotism to treat hysterical complaints. They soon realized that not only could hypnosis cure or cease such symptoms, it could also induce the same symptoms or behaviors. For example, if a hypnotized subject was told that he had no feeling in his hand, the hand could then be pricked with a needle without the subject showing any response. On the basis of such findings, Liébault and Bernheim developed the theory that hysteria was actually a form of self-hypnosis, and that other mental disorders might also be due entirely to psychological causes.

A little later, Pierre Janet (1859–1947) reasoned that hysteria was due to a splitting off from conscious experiences of certain ideas that continued to influence behavior. He noticed that under hypnosis many patients recalled upsetting events that seemed to be related to the onset of their symptoms. He found that in some cases, when patients expressed the strong feelings they had experienced at the time the original events took place, their symptoms weakened temporarily or disappeared.

Janet became interested in the process of dissociation, a mental state in which ideas, emotions, and memories are split off from the main focus of attention. Janet noticed that dissociated states may continue to function as semiautonomous influences over behavior. These states can be viewed as disturbances in the stream of consciousness that result in derangement in the way people think about and tell the stories of their lives. Janet used hypnosis as a means of integrating these split-off ideas, emotions, and memories into the mainstream of consciousness.

Once again, then, I must address the key issue. What role does consciousness play in the behavior used to diagnose a person with schizophrenia? I understand that for researchers and scientists not to be able to explain consciousness in materialistic or biological terms, it is more convenient to just ignore the subject, but people's lives are at stake. So we must take an honest look at this issue.

TWO WAYS TO VIEW THE SYMPTOMS AND BEHAVIORS ASSOCIATED WITH A DIAGNOSIS OF SCHIZOPHRENIA

So, where are we? I have illustrated that, even though biological psychiatry still believes that schizophrenia in particular is a disease caused by something like defective genes and/or chemical imbalances, certain well-credentialed researchers and professional organizations are finally admitting that those theories are not supported by causal evidence. I have also illustrated that, through the power of human consciousness, a person's mind can create almost any kind of symptom or behavior, as well as exercise considerable control over the human body. This especially includes the symptoms used to diagnose a person with schizophrenia. Finally, through examples such as the stressed-out father coming home from work, or the child bullied at school, we all can act a little "schizophrenic" at times. In addition, like the man in the coffee shop, a part of us is able to turn on and off even the strangest of behaviors. Read the following quote from John Rosen, a recognized expert in the psychotherapy of schizophrenia.

...are they [the symptoms] not rather the unrepressed manifestations of the unconscious that exists in all of us? Isn't it true that these fundamental symptoms are also found in normal people? Is there any individual free from ambivalence, disturbed affectivity and association, and a predisposition to fantasy? In the schizophrenic, to be sure, the unconscious is not controlled by the healthy resistances of the normal person and bursts forth in delusion, hallucinations, etc. Is not this difference between the normal and the schizophrenic one of degree rather than of kind? It is my belief that anyone can become schizophrenic, no matter how healthy his developmental years might have been. There is no such thing as mental health that can withstand all destructive environmental influences.[17]

Again, here is the key to both understanding the symptoms and behaviors associated with a diagnosis of schizophrenia, and the path to a healing and recovery of this condition. If examined carefully, the behaviors or symptoms are present to serve the person in a particular way. For example, one of the men at the prison where I worked often heard the voice of his grandmother and was subsequently diagnosed with schizophrenia. When I took the time to better understand this person, he shared with me that he grew up in an extremely violent and drug-infested part of his city and that both of his parents were drug addicts. In addition, when he was quite young, his father and his older brother were shot to death during a drug deal.

As a result, he spent a fair amount of time with his grandmother, who constantly tried to encourage him. Thus, when he would reach a very low, depressed state, especially while in prison, he would begin to hear the voice of his encouraging grandmother.

The point I need to make is that he just didn't hear *a* voice, but the voice of *his grandmother* and at the times when he was most discouraged. Genes and chemical imbalances cannot create such intentional behavior that can also serve a valuable purpose to the person.

Even seemingly negative or destructive voices or behaviors, when properly understood, are often present to help the person emotionally.

The following is an example that first helped me to understand this basic principle. One of my earliest clients after I had graduated from college and began my private practice shared that she often saw and felt bugs crawling on her that scared her to death. So, why would a *helping* unconscious create an illusion that actually terrified the person?

As a young child this client had been severely sexually abused by several adults. When the felt shame and sense of dirtiness would begin to surface consciously and come close to eventually destroying her, her mind would come to her rescue by creating the bugs. The fear of the fictitious bugs would then take her mind off the shame, keeping her from hurting herself and/or taking her life.

This may be an extreme example, but when the symptoms are examined closely enough (i.e., prisoner hearing the voice of his grandmother), it will soon become apparent that the symptoms serve some kind of purpose. If this purpose is not eventually understood, a healing and recovery may not be possible and psychotropic drugs will most likely be used to continue to disable the brain.

I could give you one example after another where, when I took the time and created the necessary safety, an element of intentionality and purpose existed behind the hallucinations or other behaviors and symptoms. In fact, manic behavior can and does follow along the same lines of reasoning. Read what the actress Patty Duke stated about the element of intentionality behind the manic symptoms she suffered from.

> That's the childlike part of the mania. It's whatever you
> see you want, that's it, it's yours, with no thought, not the
> slightest anxiety about what it takes to get it or how you're

going to pay for it. It really is like believing that the money's all growing on trees.

During mania, we own the world, we don't need anybody, and we don't need anything. We're going to be millionaires, and we believe it.[18]

Thus, as with the symptoms used to diagnose a person with schizophrenia, understanding the specific meaning of the symptoms associated with a person's life becomes one of the main keys to that person's recovery.

WHAT ABOUT TRUE OR ESTABLISHED CAUSES?

There are many true biologically-based conditions, such as sleep deprivation, syphilis, different forms of dementia, and drug abuse, to name a few, that can cause a person to hallucinate and/or become paranoid. Thus, a good physical exam, along with proper nutrition, sleep, and exercise, is appropriate and highly recommended. But again, the symptoms used to diagnose a person with schizophrenia in particular will have a *specific* emotional purpose, *specifically* designed by the person's unconscious to best serve that particular hurting person. Biologically-based conditions do not contain this *intentional* aspect.

ORIGIN OF THE TERM "SCHIZOPHRENIA"

At this point it may be helpful to explain just how and why the term "schizophrenia" found its way into our vocabulary.

Until the end of the 19th century, the different forms of what we now call *psychosis* were generally considered to be the result of a single disease. But after studying hundreds of subjects and their seemingly unlimited behaviors and/or symptoms, researcher Emil Kraepelin proposed the concept that there were three separate psychoses representing three separate disease entities: dementia praecox, paranoia, and manic-depressive psychosis. In reference to the condition of dementia praecox, Kraepelin believed that this illness normally began in adolescence and that it involved irreversible mental deterioration.

Within a few years after Kraepelin's dementia classification, many researchers, including Eugen Bleuler, began to realize that Kraepelin was wrong on both accounts; that indeed some individuals contracted this so-called disease later in life, and that many individuals recovered. Bleuler then proposed the adoption of a new term. Quoting directly from his writings,

> We are left with no alternative but to give the disease a new name, less apt to be misunderstood. I am well aware of the disadvantages of the proposed name but I know of no better one. I call the dementia praecox "schizophrenia" [from the Greek words schizein, meaning "to split," and phren, meaning "mind"] because the "splitting" of the different psychic functions is one of its most important characteristics.[19]

Because of the dissatisfaction of Kraepelin's term *dementia praecox*, Bleuler began to search for a better understanding of this condition. To do so, he enlisted help from some bright young physicians. To begin this investigation, in 1900 he sent Franz Riklin to Heidelberg to learn about the association testing that Kraepelin was using in his laboratory.

It was also at about this same time that right after graduating from medical school, Carl Jung arrived at the clinic Bleuler was directing to help him with his research. When Riklin returned from Heidelberg, he and Jung began developing their own word-association tests. Quoting from an article by Moskowitz,

> They set about their task, which Bleuler hoped would inform his developing theory, systematically—first recording the associations of non-psychiatric subjects under a range of conditions before moving on to psychiatric subjects. Their

studies formed the basis for a series of publications in the early 1900s, ultimately released in book form under the title of Diagnostic Association Studies. During the course of these studies, which diverged from prior associational research by focusing not only on the time delay between the stimulus word and its response, but also on the personal meaning of the response and whether the subject could recall their response on subsequent trials, Jung developed the concept of a feeling-toned or emotionally-charged complex. This important concept... was to become central to Bleuler's developing concept of schizophrenia. [20]

In the application of word-association tests, a subject is given a word, and then the investigator records such data as the time delay between when the word is given and the person's response, as well as the possible personal meaning of the response.

I mentioned earlier the father who had brought in his son who had been living and prostituting himself on the streets of Hollywood. "Hollywood" would obviously not be a term Jung would have used, but it can represent a fairly neutral word for one individual and obviously a trigger word for this young man.

So if I presented that word to a person who had lived his entire life in New York and had no strong emotional connection to Hollywood, he may respond with, "Oh, a place where movie stars live." In addition, he may take a quick moment or two to think how he may want to respond, since he had no strong emotional connection to the place. But when I mentioned the word "Hollywood" to my client, he almost instantly began to talk about the "light of Jesus."

Along the same lines, when I ask a person in therapy an emotionally-charged question, and that person is not ready to give me a truthful response or is incapable of doing so, I will usually receive one of three responses. The person will (a) give me a very quick, superficial response, (b) just not answer me, or (c) change the subject.

In such a situation, the person is not necessarily deliberately acting dishonestly. The unconscious part of his or her mind quickly takes over before any painful feelings can surface, resulting in a response that helps push the feelings back down before they can fully surface. These kinds of behaviors are what Jung referred to as a "feeling-toned or emotionally-charged complex." Thus, to me, what Bleuler identified as the "splitting of the different psychic functions" is no more than the person's mind running off or hiding from the powerful and terrifying feelings locked up or dissociated off from the person.

Consequently, as Bleuler and Jung used a *non-medical, non-biological* test to notice that certain words triggered an emotionally reactive response resulting in abnormal, often bizarre behavior and thoughts, Bleuler searched diligently for the proper term to describe such behavior and came up with the term *schizophrenia*.

THE PROCESS, A CLOSER LOOK

Let me now see if I can explain the process leading up to a possible diagnosis of schizophrenia in terms of what kinds of life encounters any of us can experience.

I am sure you have been in a situation where you have had to push down a violating event, and then tried to hold it down, both emotionally and cognitively. Yet, as you did, there was another part of you that just wanted to let loose, perhaps scream out, throw something, or lie down on the floor and have a good temper tantrum. Again, maybe someone at work insulted or embarrassed you in an unfair way. Or, perhaps on the way home, some driver was extremely rude to you.

There are times when, cognitively or rationally, we know that such acting out behavior is not safe or acceptable, so we attempt to suppress the energy behind it. But then either this energy becomes too intense to continue to hold down or, if it is suddenly triggered, this energy quickly surfaces in some form. The release can surface in one of two ways. Either the stored-up feelings can come rushing up to the surface or, in order to keep the pain further suppressed, the person's mind may split completely away from the feelings, creating a new reality.

Let's go back to the young kid from Hollywood who had to prostitute himself to survive. As a result, he was full of shame and self-hate. To manage the intensity of this self-hate that literally could emotionally eat him alive, he had to dissociate or create a new (schizophrenic) mental state.

What happens when we become bored? Although boredom brings only minor discomfort, it is nevertheless a pain that we can't endure for very long. After a few minutes, our minds will take off, searching for something else to focus on (i.e., food) as a way of dissociating from that pain.

The pain of boredom is usually small enough that, when necessary (in a class lecture for example), we can easily bring our minds back, canceling out or overpowering the need to dissociate.

But for the kid from Hollywood, he was not just dealing with a little bit of boredom. He needed to manage the shame and hurt of knowing that he chose to climb into the back seat of a car and allow strangers to do whatever they wanted with his body. Thus, when he had to split to stay away from this intense shame, he needed to also create a new reality (Jesus shining His light down on him).

But think for a moment. If we are at work, in a lecture, or at a meeting, and we are becoming bored, and we then create a fantasy of what we will eat or do when we get home, are we not mentally doing the same thing?

Do you understand why, after so many years of research, no actual cause and effect or pathophysiological evidence has ever been found? There are some brain differences that are measurable at times—shrinking of parts of the brain, an increase in the size of the ventricles, etc. But all of these differences can easily be explained by the effects of either prolonged stress upon the body and/or the use of psychotropic drugs. And for the kid from Hollywood, you can just imagine the stress he must have put himself through, trying to survive emotionally and physically as he prostituted himself.

THE DIFFERENCE BETWEEN A *SCHIZOPHRENIC BREAK* AND THE CONDITION REFERRED TO AS *SCHIZOPHRENIA*

The truth is that there is no biological cause-and-effect defective difference between splitting because of boredom, having an angry outburst, or what we professionals refer to as psychotic behavior. If I am bored and must split from the moment to jump to something pleasurable, to me that is just a small "schizophrenic moment." But for someone like the Hollywood kid, an ongoing, more consistent pattern needed to be developed. Or, like the one prisoner who, when depressed and discouraged, he would begin to hear the voice of his grandmother. To divert his mind from these painful feelings, his mind had learned how to create the belief in this voice the moment he began to feel overwhelmed with his loneliness and desperateness. By almost instantly creating the voice (or, in the case of the Hollywood kid, seeing the light of Jesus, etc.), the painful feelings are never fully experienced.

Thus, until a proper healing and recovery program is instituted, these behaviors will continue to be needed to survive emotionally.

As a final illustration, allow me to share an example that I like to use from Bert Karon's excellent article titled "The Tragedy of Schizophrenia."[21] For several decades, Dr. Karon has been teaching graduate students at a major university the art of psychotherapy with individuals diagnosed with schizophrenia. Working with a person diagnosed with schizophrenia, he stated,

The best description of what it feels like to be schizophrenic came from a catatonic man whom it took 8 weeks of psychotherapy (without medication) to get out of the hospital and back to work. One of his symptoms was bowing. When asked why he bowed, he said,

> *"I don't bow."*
>
> *"Yes, you do."*
>
> *"No, I don't bow."*
>
> *"Wait a minute. You do this [the therapist bowed]. This is bowing; you bow."*
>
> *"No, I don't bow."*
>
> *"But you do this."*
>
> *"That's not bowing."*
>
> *"What is it?"*
>
> *"It's balancing."*
>
> *"What are you balancing?"*
>
> *"Emotions."*
>
> *"What emotions?"*
>
> *"Fear and loneliness."*

That is, when he was lonely, he wanted to get close to people (so he leaned forward). When he got close to people, he got scared and had to pull away (so he straightened up). But then he was lonely again.

Balancing between fear and loneliness is the best description of what it feels like to be schizophrenic. That we do not want to understand this is a tragedy.[22]

In summary, notice the broad range of symptoms and/or behaviors that I have included so far in the few examples that I have used. They include:

Grandmother's voice
Light of Jesus
Crippled hand
Rocking
Blindness
Talking to a fictitious person

TY C. COLBERT | 39

Running naked down the street
Fictitious bugs

This is why we can't simply start with a person's behavior or symptoms, apply a diagnosis of some sort, and then attempt to drug the symptoms away. Each person's situation will be unique as to the type and amount of emotional pain, the way that emotional pain is dissociated off, and then how it later resurfaces in the form of specific behaviors and symptoms.

The solution then becomes the identification, healing, and recovery from those painful experiences. Finishing a boring task, arriving home, taking a warm shower, then eating a good meal is the process of healing and recovering from a hard day's work. Even though the basic principle is much the same, for those diagnosed with schizophrenia, the process will be a little more difficult, to say the least. This will be the topic of Part II. But before we start a discussion on the healing and recovery process, I need to include a few words about the use of psychotropic drugs.

PSYCHOTROPIC DRUGS

At the end of this book, I offer additional resources. But let's quickly review a few points regarding the topic of psychotropic drugs.

1. It is admitted by the American Psychiatric Association and the British Psychological Association that no chemical imbalances have ever been found to cause the symptoms associated with a diagnosis of schizophrenia.

2. Once again, according to Steven Hyman, the past director of the NIMH, psychotropic drugs work basically the same as street drugs by disabling the brain, thus cutting the person off from full awareness of his or her feelings.

3. These drugs, even the newer ones, can cause severe damage to the biology of the person because these drugs achieve their effectiveness, again, by their physically disabling effect.[23,24]

4. Because of a person's out-of-control thoughts and emotions, these drugs can serve a useful purpose. On the other hand, if at all possible, the ultimate goal should not be one of drug dependence, but one of minimizing and/or eliminating the use of these substances through a proper healing and recovery program.

A STRONG WORD OF CAUTION

With the above said about the use of psychotropic drugs, *do not* begin to withdraw from these substances without first participating in a healing and recovery program and with proper medical supervision. Withdrawing from any psychotropic substances can become life-threatening, and at the very least, set a person's recovery program back several months or even years. Also, refer to "Additional Resources" at the end of this book for more information on the proper withdrawing of these substances.

SUMMARY OF PART I

Before I summarize what I have covered so far, let me assure you that these ideas and principles are not just mine. This is information I have gathered from highly respected professionals and organizations over the past 35 years. I mentioned earlier *The International Society for Psychological and Social Approaches to Psychosis*, a 55-year-old worldwide organization consisting of psychiatrists, medical doctors, psychologists, researchers, and recovered individuals, all of whom believe that recovery

TY C. COLBERT | 41

and healing are more than possible. Take a look at their website at *www.isps.org*, making note of the multitude of books that members have written on the topic of a non-biological, healing, and recovery model. Three other professional organizations worth examining are these: *www.psyintegraty. com, madinamerica.com, and breggin.com.*

Let me now quickly summarize what I have covered.

* With over 100 years of research, no biological cause-and-effect, pathophysiological evidence exists for the condition referred to as schizophrenia. Granted, there are many theories; but nothing has been proven. This fact is freely acknowledged by the National Institute of Mental Health.[25]

* Psychotropic drugs do not correct a defect or imbalance but work temporarily by disabling the brain.

* As I will illustrate in Part II, recovery and healing are more than possible. The process may involve hard work, but recovery is an established fact.

* Any individual, when feeling violated and/or overwhelmed with powerful negative feelings and life experiences, can act "weird" or "bizarre" at times. At such a point, the suffering individual needs the help of others to heal or recover from such moments (whether from a bad day at work or severe abuse) to successfully move forward in his or her life.

With this introduction to the topic of schizophrenia behind us, let us now look at what a healing and recovery program can entail.

PART II

A Basic Understanding of the "Necessary" Healing and Recovery Process

THE MAIN GOAL IN PART I WAS to present a short, concise, and easy-to-understand explanation of the condition referred to as *schizophrenia*. Part II now presents an overview of the healing and recovery process. My goal is not to take the suffering individual through an actual step-by-step process, because that can possibly be a lengthy journey for some individuals. But my hope and prayer is that by providing an overall understanding of the process, the person and his or her helpers can then begin a successful journey, making the necessary adjustments along the way. In fact, the more I can put the suffering person in charge of his or her own program, along with the still-needed help from others, the more successful will be the outcome for all.

RECOVERY IS MORE THAN POSSIBLE

In my book and workbook, *Healing Runaway Minds* and *From Breakdown to Breakthrough*, I spent considerable time presenting examples and studies illustrating that full recovery is more than possible. Because my desire is to keep this book as brief as possible, let me share just one program that is showing considerable success worldwide, the Open Dialogue Treatment approach.

Western Lapland in Finland was receiving some of the worst outcomes for schizophrenia in all of Europe. But through a program called Open Dialogue Treatment (ODT), they are now obtaining perhaps some of the best results in the world. ODT's main approach is to place the primary form of care on developing a social network of family and helpers, involving the patient in all treatment decisions.

In a five-year follow-up study, 86% of the patients have returned to their jobs or studies as students, or have been seeking employment, thus not receiving government disability. In the same study, 82% did not have residual psychotic symptoms.[26] Official government statistics comparing 22 health districts in Finland found that the district using ODT was the only one not to have any new chronic hospital patients in a two-year period.[27] What is it they're doing right?

With first-episode cases involving a psychotic break, an ODT team intervenes either in the home or at their clinic, with the goal of establishing a dialogue with the patient, providing immediate help, and organizing a treatment meeting within 24 hours of the initial contact. They prefer to meet in people's homes, both at first and with ongoing help, but they will use their clinic/hospital if necessary, mainly if safety concerns are an issue.

ODT views psychosis and schizophrenia as "happening between people, not within a person." They see the problem, not in the person's biology, but in the network of relationships surrounding the life of the person who is "in crisis."

Quoting directly from the ODT website,

> *The basic vehicle of Open Dialogue* is its radically altered version of the treatment meeting. As soon as possible in

a given situation, the team, which consists of at least two clinicians, gathers everyone connected to the crisis, including the person at the center, their family and social network, all professional helpers, and anyone else closely involved. There are no separate staff meetings to talk about the "case." Rather all discussion and any decisions about medication and hospitalization take place with everyone present.

The aim of the treatment meeting is to generate dialogue that leads to common understandings, which become the basis of care. It begins first by eliciting the point of view of the person who has the overt symptoms. Often there is a special kind of meticulous back-and-forth exchange between this person and the therapists to develop a more lucid way of expressing the situation and create a shared language. Building on this interaction, the therapists weave a common understanding of the crisis by bringing forward the voice of each of the participants. The exchange of voices creates a new fabric of meaning and engagement to which everyone has contributed important threads.[28]

So, what are the keys to this highly successful program?

1. They view the recovery as relational or "happening between people," not a person's biology. Remember Dan Fisher? Once out of the hospital, he soon realized that his diagnosis of schizophrenia had more to do with personal issues or the way he had developed unhealthy relationships.

2. Instead of a doctor almost instantly deciding that he or she is an expert in a person's life and all that is required is to prescribe the correct drug, a team approach is used that includes family members and anyone else close to the suffering person.

3. The goal or aim is not to suppress the symptoms with drugs, but to "generate a dialogue" between and/or among the key persons.

4. The first step in generating such a dialogue is to "elicit the point of view of the person who has the overt symptoms."

In other words, instead of simply starting with the symptoms, coming up with a diagnosis, then applying a drug, the first step is to learn about the person and his or her personal struggle and inner life. (At times a drug may be used, but only to calm the person down, with the goal of eventually minimizing and/or eliminating the use of drugs.)

Once a common understanding of the crisis has been obtained, a more personalized recovery program is developed.

Let me reduce this most successful program down a little more.

1. It's about relationships, not biology.

2. It requires the interaction and help of others.

3. The person's emotional pain must eventually be identified and understood in order to help him or her help themselves.

4. These individuals are "recovering," not just stabilized on a regimen of psychiatric drugs.

THE BASIC PROBLEM AND SOLUTION

For additional clarity, let's go back to the basic problem as I have defined it. To do so clearly, I will make use of the following diagram.

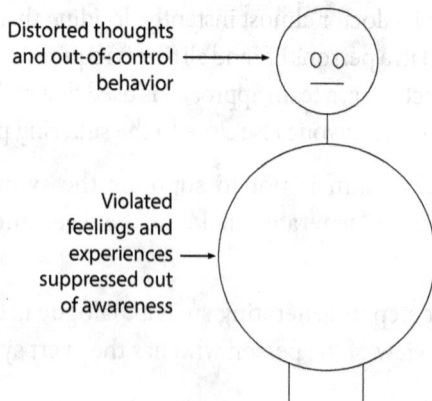

Distorted thoughts and out-of-control behavior

Violated feelings and experiences suppressed out of awareness

In any felt violation to our selfhood, feelings such as hurt, loneliness, anger, rage, shame, and/or guilt will result. Just as boredom is an uncomfortable feeling and one for which our minds will come to our rescue and attempt to divert our attention, so our minds will attempt to divert or dissociate away other, more painful feelings.

Our minds come to our rescue in one of two basic ways. If the feelings associated with an event are strong and overpowering, our mind has the ability to completely deny or shut us off from full awareness. The World War II soldier with the crippled hand is a prime example. Children and, at times, adults subjected to severe forms of abuse will block out painful experiences to some extent.

The other main defense occurs when our minds attempt to distort the circumstances to the degree needed. For example, let's say someone embarrassed you or verbally violated you at work. The trauma most likely is not great enough that your mind must dissociate or separate from the experience, but your mind (partially subconsciously) may quickly come to your rescue by finding fault with that person in the attempt to minimize the felt intensity of the violation. Or, in the case of someone who has had his or her trust violated quite often, a more generalized paranoia toward certain situations or individuals may result.

With our Hollywood kid, for example, because of the severity of the abuse, he needed to both dissociate off the pain and use his mind to create an illusion of the presence of Jesus. In fact, it was the creation of this illusion that helped him to mentally dissociate from his pain. It gave him something else to focus on, as any of us often do when bored.

When I went partially blind during the times I was lecturing, I did not distort the situation or people who were present, but my mind did, in a sense, distort my ability to be aware.

I am sure individuals can come up with other types of defenses, but (a) dissociating away the awareness of certain events and the corresponding feelings, and (b) mentally distorting the reality of the situation or others will be sufficient in order for us to develop an overall healing and recovery program. But before we start, again take note that these two primary defenses are used by everyone, not just a person diagnosed with schizophrenia. It is only when they take on certain extreme forms that my profession rushes in and gives that person a diagnosis.

AN OVERVIEW OF THE PLAN

Here is our healing and recovery plan in its most elementary form for the suffering person:

1. Begin to entertain that certain behaviors or thoughts appear non-productive or troublesome.

2. Obtain a proper physical and/or adjust one's diet and level of exercise to make sure no true biological conditions are involved. Even if symptoms are primarily emotionally based, not sleeping or eating well can exacerbate the present symptoms and recovery process.

3. If the behaviors are too out of control or dangerous to the suffering person or others, some psychotropic medication may be needed. But the main goal should be one of working hard on a recovery and healing program to eventually minimize or, better yet, eliminate the need for these disabling, toxic substances.

4. Begin to take an honest look at why, unconsciously, the person's mind needed to (a) dissociate, and (b) create troublesome, non-productive, but *protective* behaviors.

Once again, is this not the basic healing and growth process we all will need to go through in our attempt to mature emotionally as responsible and self-fulfilling adults? I am in my 70s, and I still struggle along these same lines at times when facing new life challenges.

A MAJOR EVENT VERSUS AN ONGOING MINOR EVENTS

To further clarify the possible causes of a psychotic break or the ongoing condition referred to as schizophrenia, let me compare two types of events: major violating events and a series of smaller, but still violating events.

1. Major events. The kid who prostituted himself on the streets of Hollywood would certainly qualify as having experienced a major traumatic event. In addition, severe childhood abuse is often the root cause of a psychotic break or a later diagnosis of schizophrenia. When I was working as a prison psychologist, I encountered several situations where an inmate had been in and out of prison for most of his life and also had been given a diagnosis of schizophrenia. When such a situation would arise, I would then ask the inmate if he had been sexually abused as a child. As hard as it was for them to admit to such abuse, they would answer "Yes" about 80% of the time.

But let me make it clear that a break from reality does not always result from major abuse in a person's childhood. Tragic events, especially in times of war, can result in the person's mind needing to take over unconsciously. The World War II soldier with the crippled hand is one example. Tom Hanks, in the movie *Saving Private Ryan,* dissociated from reality (psychotic break) for a short time when he witnessed the carnage during the D-Day invasion of France.

My youngest son recently moved out to live and attend college in a different state. His mother and I both had difficulty adjusting for a short time. I remember sitting in my front yard not long after he left and sensing my mind's desire to distort the circumstances. There was a part of me that wanted (needed) to believe that if I just sat there long enough, he would come driving around that corner in his car.

When I took some time to pay attention to my body, I could feel the pain of the loneliness of his not coming home that evening or anytime soon. Thus it was most obvious to me that my distorted thinking was not the result of some defect, but a way that my mind was acting in a "creative" way, attempting to minimize my pain in the only way it knew how to.

If I would have also had other major abandonment issues or events in my life, my beliefs and corresponding behavior might have become even more distorted. I might have started telling the neighbors that I saw his car drive by or that God told me my son would soon return.

Obviously, we all can find ourselves at the mercy of unexpected painful events and not know how to take care of ourselves emotionally.

2. *Ongoing series of minor events.* Growing up as a teenager can result in a very stressful time in a person's life, especially today. I graduated from high school in a relatively small town in 1960. I have worked with high school kids for the last 40-plus years. When I was a teen, we certainly were subjected to peer pressure and the push to succeed, but I truly believe the stress on teens today is much greater.

I don't want to go into much of a discussion here, but I will state that even though the pain may not be that great (incest vs. peer pressure), many kids grow up today in a semi-dissociative or trance-like state, suppressing too much pain over a lengthy period. In addition, many kids today unfortunately hate themselves, their looks or parts of their bodies, their nationality, and even their parents. They may not be fully aware of this self-hate or self-judgment, but it is present and is an ongoing, destructive force. Again, they may not be that aware, but this lack of awareness adds to the dissociating process, setting a person up for a possible psychotic break, an episode of depression, and so forth.

So, let's not make it too big a mystery when a person growing up begins to show problems related to emotional stress. Sure, each person will have his or her own story to uncover, but let's also admit that whether it is alcohol or drug dependency, depression, anxiety, dropping out of school, or a possible break from reality, all of these behaviors relate to a suffering person's cry for help. In fact, getting drunk or high on drugs usually represents a need to escape a present reality in order to create a new one.

THE EMOTIONAL PAIN, HEALING, AND RECOVERY DIAGRAM AND PROCESS

To best explain the required healing and recovery process, allow me to introduce you to the following diagram. Before we start, remember that the main goal is to overcome the effects of the trauma in a person's life, whether that may have been a major event such as incest, or a series of minor events such as feeling abandoned or teased growing up. Once again, there is absolutely no conclusive cause-and-effect evidence illustrating that the symptoms associated with a diagnosis of schizophrenia are the result of some biological defect.

The following diagram will be used to explain the basic different treatment modalities.

Violation	Terror	Hurt Loneliness	Anger Guilt	Rage Shame	Mind running away	Symptoms Behaviors	Diagnosis

Drug therapy

Cognitive therapy

Twelve-step recovery work

In-depth healing and recovery work

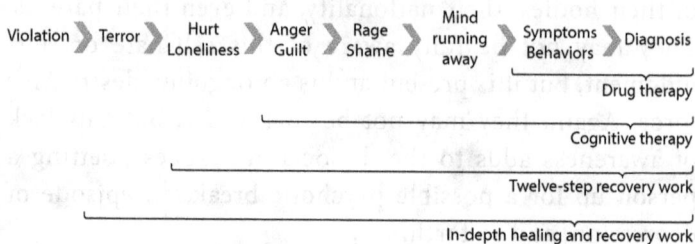

Let's start with the top part. When a person is first violated, or after the first felt violation, there is always an element of terror involved. This element may be so small that our minds can quickly dissociate from it, but it is present. If you were to start making fun of a child in front of his peers, you would see the corresponding terror on his face. Likewise, a worker suddenly called into his supervisor's office for disciplinary reasons will experience some element of terror.

Since terror is the most uncomfortable negative feeling of all, our bodies and minds will begin to take over as quickly as possible to push down the terror by first turning the terror into hurt and loneliness. These are also uncomfortable feelings, but much easier to manage. With the feelings of hurt and loneliness, our minds can begin to look for solutions. We may turn the hurt into anger or judgments towards others, or, in the case of loneliness, we may look for companionship. But terror is a naked feeling that we are forced to just sit with unless we can transform it by purposely and often unconsciously changing the reality of a situation.

But also because the feelings of hurt and loneliness are uncomfortable, the feelings or emotions of anger, guilt, rage, and shame eventually emerge. Finally, if there are a number of violating events that are at least partially suppressed out of awareness, eventually the symptoms associated with a "mental illness" will emerge. Once the symptoms surface, then a diagnosis can be given and a so-called disease possibly assumed.

To help you better understand that this is the same basic sequence that can lead to any number of diagnoses, including schizophrenia, let's first re-examine the example of the kid who was bullied at school. Let's also assume that he got into trouble for acting out at school, and later for picking on his sister. The following is a diagram of his emotional sequence of events.

Violation (bullied)	Small amount of terror	Hurt by people and felt alone	Anger rage suppressed	Acted out towards others	Possible diagnosis

A possible diagnosis for this child could be ADHD, oppositional defiant behavior, or conduct disorder. In fact, in December 2015, I ran across an article stating that in 2014, almost 20,000 prescriptions for antipsychotic medications were written for children under the age of two, mostly for hard-to-control or acting-out behaviors.[29]

What, then, would be the best way to help this child? There are two basic approaches: a disease, biological, drug approach or a relational approach. This child could be given a formal diagnosis of some sort and a corresponding drug to help subdue his acting-out behavior, or someone could take the time to understand what is "uniquely" going on or troubling him. In summary, as oversimplified as this explanation may appear, these are the two basic choices, regardless of the behavior, symptoms, or diagnosis.

DIFFERENT TREATMENT MODALITIES

Let's now return to the preceding diagram to focus on the bottom half, the various basic treatment modalities.

A. *Drug therapy.* Again, drugs work by disabling the brain, shutting the person off from his or her deeper emotional pain.

The drugs, in essence, work the same as street drugs or alcohol. Consequently, there is no healing and very little personal growth taking place.

For example, let's assume a father has had a rough day at work, and to handle (or suppress) his pain he has a few drinks at home. Such an approach may work a few times, but there is no healing from his daily pain. Eventually he will relapse, possibly act out toward his family, develop physical problems, and so forth. Yet, this is the same approach as giving the child who is bullied at school a drug to attempt to keep his behavior in check.

B. Twelve-Step recovery work. I want to cover this one next because, in some ways, it is an easier one to understand. Any of us are susceptible to becoming out of control with some of our behavior, especially when it involves such substances as alcohol, drugs, food, sex, or any other substance or activity that can bring a sense of instant gratification. The instant gratification helps to neutralize our overpowering negative feelings. Thus, our mind will become very tricky along these lines. The unconscious part of our mind will begin to anticipate the surfacing of our pain. To take our mind off the pain before it surfaces, our unconscious will refocus on something pleasurable like alcohol. In fact, instead of feeling the pain, our mind will insert a craving and then attempt to justify having just "one drink," "one piece of cake," and so forth.

A twelve-step program is one with a set of guiding principles outlining a course of action for an individual's recovery from addiction, compulsion, or other behavioral problems. Originally developed for individuals with an alcohol dependency or addiction, the program has expanded to other compulsive or addictive issues such as narcotics, gambling, food, sex, hoarding, co-dependency, and spending problems.

Here is a story that I shared in my book *Healing Runaway Minds*. This person was a recovering alcoholic who had been in therapy with me and was doing quite well. But one of the issues that we still had not worked on in any depth was the verbal shaming abuse he had received from his father growing up. In addition, although we did not recognize it at the time, his boss would often shame him in much the same way as his father had.

One particular afternoon, his boss threw a shaming comment at him after what had already been a stressful day. When he got off work and began to drive home, his unconscious clicked into action. He suddenly started thinking about a bar where he used to hang out. The more he thought about this bar, the more he felt an urge—an actual bodily sensation—to drive past this bar to see if any of his friends' cars were out front. He reasoned that if he saw any of his friends' cars, he would stop to visit, but would not have a drink. Even knowing that just driving by his old bar would put his sobriety at risk, his mind tried to convince him that he would be safe. "Oh, I won't have a drink, or maybe only one. I just want to see my old friends. I'll be okay." Of course, if he had one drink, it would most likely lead to another, then another. Instead, he called me and as we talked on the phone, we were able to form the connection between his boss and his father for the first time. Shortly after that, he found a new place to work, one with a much more supportive, non-shaming supervisor. He also made a more solid commitment to his recovery program.

C. *Cognitive therapy.* When violated, our minds will take off and can become quite irrational, delusional, fearful, and so forth. Again, go back to the young man who prostituted himself on the streets of Hollywood. His mind needed to run off in an extreme way to suppress the intense shame he felt for how he chose to use his body. The truth is that anytime we experience a few painful events, our minds can take off on us in an effort to find some solution to the growing pain. For example, if we are having a bad day and are late to an appointment, and on top of that, we keep hitting one red traffic light after another, we may begin to think God is punishing us or that life is against us for some reason. A cognitive approach can help individuals regain control over their out-of-control thoughts as well as their feelings. For example, let's say I am late for an important appointment and I am stuck in extremely heavy traffic. The "small" fear (terror) of being late will send my mind turning. But by regaining control of my thoughts, I can counteract that belief by telling myself, "It's not the end of the world if I am late. It's not my fault, and I am still an okay person." If the fear of being late or the consequences of being late are not that great, then with some proper "cognitive" or positive thought processing, I hopefully can calm myself down.

D. *In-depth healing and grief work.* I mentioned earlier my work with prisoners who had been sexually abused as children, were later diagnosed with schizophrenia, and were then in and out of prison for most of their adult lives. Once they were willing to admit to and share about their abuse in our groups, cry and express anger at times, and struggle with why a trusted adult would abuse them in such a way, a more formal and in-depth healing process would take place. As a result, after being in prison for much of their adult lives, once released these men did not return.

Perhaps the most important point to understand with in-depth healing and recovery work is this: If the pain that is set off is too great, mainly from unhealed past events, then cognitive therapy alone will not necessarily be the best approach. Why? Because a formal healing of those past events (or parts of the person) needs to take place.

Let's go back to the incest survivor groups that I ran in prison. When I started working as a psychologist in the prison system, two inmates I interviewed told me they had been in and out of prison their entire lives. One had been in prison almost 40 different times. The other one, age 42, had been in prison for all but 18 months of his life, from age 18 to the present.

I was shocked because these two individuals were not in prison for some serious crime, but for stealing and the unlawful possession of a drug, often to support a drug habit or to feed themselves when homeless. Again, when I inquired further, both of them had been sexually abused as children. In addition, they had been given plenty of psychological care consisting mainly of drugs and cognitive-based talk therapy, but they had never been helped to heal from these wounds. Thus, whenever their deeper, cut-off feelings of shame, anger, and loneliness were triggered, they found themselves helpless to control their behavior, and unfortunately they landed back in prison. As a result of these two men sharing their stories, I started a group for inmates who had been sexually abused. In the group, we focused on bringing up their pain, sharing it, crying at times, expressing anger if appropriate, telling each other we cared for each other, hugging when appropriate, and so forth.

What were the results? Again, these men stopped returning to prison. They were finally given a chance to re-experience their original pain with a caring and affirming confidential group. They had all been in and out of prison for over 20 years, and during that time, they had *never* been given the chance to mourn their past emotional wounds. Psychotropic medications did not help because they worked the same as street drugs, suppressing the pain and making them "crazier" at times when their suppressed pain was suddenly triggered. Some cognitive therapy helped a little, but they still could not control their pain and especially their rage *without the healing of the events*. Twelve-step programs did help with those individuals who took the program seriously, but that program would also fail without the inner healing of their past emotional wounds.

A COMBINATION OF ALL FOUR TREATMENTS

The men in my incest survivor groups had been seriously abused and violated, especially as children. Besides the sexual abuse, most of them had been physically abused by an adult as well as emotionally and verbally abused. In addition, due to the intense shame of the abuse ("Why was I chosen?" or "What was wrong (bad) with me?"), they had emotionally degraded themselves for years. Finally, they had to somehow handle the shame and guilt of being in and out of prison for most of their lives, disappointing their loved ones along the way. Yet, after years of prison and criminal life, they were now putting together successful lives.

How were they accomplishing this? They were doing so by appropriately using the four individual major treatment modalities presented in the diagram. The vast majority of them were not using any psychotropic medications, in part because they had attempted in the past to manage their pain by using these drugs as well as street drugs. But the ones who did need some help used psychotropic drugs sparingly. And because they were serious about their total healing and recovery program, they were using the drugs appropriately, most often when they felt too out of control to manage their own emotions, especially in a prison setting.

Many of them were also working a Twelve-Step recovery program; and the ones who did, benefited greatly. A tremendous amount of wisdom results from a commitment to this program. In fact, those who fully participated were often teaching me something valuable about recovery.

In our group, I mainly focused on in-depth healing and grief work. In the safety of the group, I wanted the men to experience the very depths of their suppressed pain. In addition, many of the men were using several cognitive-oriented materials. Some of this material included religious writings or sayings, positive affirmation books, daily positive messages, and so forth.

In general, the more severe the past violations or the more out of control the behavior and thoughts, the more complete and multidimensional a recovery and healing program needs to be.

SOME EXAMPLES

With the above short introduction to the different therapeutic modalities, let's now look at some additional examples taken from my other books. The first two fortunately resulted in fairly easy solutions. As I go through these examples, notice how we (the suffering person and I) approached therapy either from a *feeling* level or a *cognitive/thought* level, as depicted by the earlier stick figure.

Example 1: 20-Year-Old, Third-Year College Student

This young lady was away from home attending college for the first time in her life when she suddenly experienced a psychotic break, resulting in some very unusual and bizarre behavior. Her roommate called the campus police, who then hospitalized her. She was put on medication and eventually released to her parents.

In order to maintain confidentiality, I will not share any of the specifics of her behavior, but I am confident that she experienced a manic/psychotic episode. I do not know what diagnosis the doctor at the hospital gave her. Again, a particular diagnosis makes little or no difference to me. My focus is on the underlying emotional pain that is driving the person's thoughts and behaviors.

She suffered from a couple of major personal image issues, including a fear of not being accepted, or of not being good enough to be likeable and attractive to the opposite sex. She had been suppressing this poor self-image (self-hate) sense of herself for several years. The corresponding feelings simply came rushing up and out soon after going away to college.

This case was fairly easy, mainly because she was quite embarrassed over her behavior and was not in denial of the fact that she had had an emotional breakdown. She had a little trouble talking about it at first, and I could sense her denial wanting to set in, so I made sure that my approach was a very gentle one. Outside of her sensitivity and embarrassment, she was quite open to help. She wanted to be able to return to college as soon as possible.

This young woman did have good support and open communication with her college roommate, who had previously participated in professional counseling. Being able to talk freely about her personal issues and her emotional breakdown with her roommate would be of great benefit and protection upon her return.

This client was quite aware of most of her feelings and was willing to admit that she had poor self-image issues. Where I needed to assist her the most was to help her become her own best *detective* and begin to understand the emotional (feeling) buildup prior to her psychotic or manic episode, as shown by the following diagram.

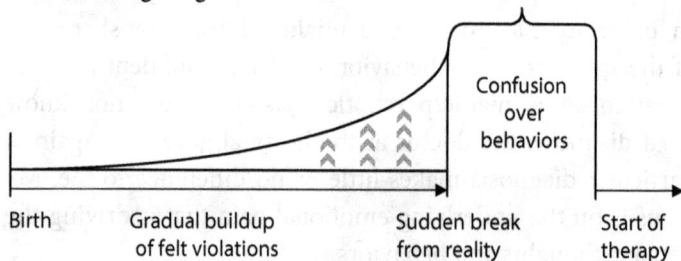

| Birth | Gradual buildup of felt violations | Sudden break from reality | Start of therapy |

As I explained to her and her parents, a psychotic break does not just come out of nowhere. There is always a series of violating events that have been suppressed over time that build up until they overwhelm the person. The detective work that needs to be done is to learn how to recognize the buildup and then seek the appropriate help before the next breakdown, episode, or relapse.

In short, this person needed to become more aware of the unconscious aspect of her life as well. She needed to learn how to become aware of the specific buildup of her feelings prior to her acting out, much as an addict is asked to identify emotional triggers.

When you approach mental illness from the viewpoint of an emotional pain perspective, there is not much difference between psychosis, drug addiction, manic behavior, or a sudden angry outburst. There are major differences in the behavior or symptoms, of course, but not in what causes the behavior, which is always *suppressed emotional pain unique to that individual.*

Example 2: Major Back Injury Resulting in Psychosis

This individual had suffered from a severe back injury and was forced to be a stay-at-home father while his wife worked. Because of his handicap, he believed he had become quite useless to his family, and he believed others viewed him this way as well.

After several years of feeling worthless as a husband and father, he experienced a psychotic break and attempted to take his own life by overdosing on his pain medication. He was hospitalized and put on an antipsychotic medication. The mind-numbing effects of the drug made him feel even more out of control and worthless because he could now barely take care of his children, much less work part-time out of his home.

A few weeks prior to his psychotic break from reality, he began receiving thoughts in his head that told him he was worthless as an individual and that taking his own life could best help his family. It was primarily because of this condition (external thoughts, paranoia) that he was given the diagnosis of paranoid schizophrenia and put on medication.

He entered therapy with me in part because he did not want to be on the medication. Our first project was to figure out what the buildup was about. The buildup actually started back in his childhood when he did not fit in well with others, resulting in feelings of worthlessness and a generalized fear of other people. Part of the reason for his feelings of worthlessness resulted from his being overweight and consequently teased about it.

He eventually teamed up with another kid who had also been ridiculed growing up, and they both began to play a mental game of "us against the world." They were both quite intelligent, and as the two reached high school, they spent many hours living in their heads, highly critical of government operations, the police, school personnel, or any adult in a position of authority. The hours they spent criticizing the external world was their best way of feeling worthwhile and empowered. Unfortunately, such isolation soon resulted in a generalized paranoia towards most adults and life in general.

There was also a very well-defined set of circumstances that led to this man's break from reality. He had reached the point where he hated himself and his life so much that he did not want to live, but he did not dare admit this to himself or his wife. So his unconscious came to his rescue and created a set of beliefs and thoughts (not quite auditory hallucinations) that convinced him that his family would be better off if he was dead.

Let me summarize this a second time because it is a very important example. In his case there was a gradual buildup of self-hate and a corresponding fear and hatred of others over the years. Getting married and supporting a family appeared to temporarily solve the problem or suppress these feelings. Then he hurt his back, and his main source of usefulness suddenly disappeared. Finally, he unconsciously reached the point where he hated himself so much that he wanted to die. But consciously (in connection with his truth feelings) he could not allow himself to take his own life. So he was stuck. He hated himself and wanted to die but could not consciously justify doing that to his family.

This internal battle was destroying him emotionally and there was no solution in sight. So his unconscious, thinking *only* of the survival of his selfhood, came up with a *brilliant* solution: It convinced him that by taking his own life, he would be doing his family a favor and he would also be rescued from his painful self-image feelings. Because he had a very strong rational side, the only way this plan would work would be if he broke completely from reality in the form of a psychotic state.

Luckily, when he began treatment, his self-awareness and dedication to his family allowed him to go right to work to learn about his past gradual emotional buildup. Most clients go through an interim period during which the therapist must help them accept the fact that they actually experienced a psychotic break, and show them that there were very specific emotional reasons that led up to the break. He systematically attacked his situation from the start of therapy.

However, his unconscious was still hard at work, and with painful events continuing to take place in his life, a buildup occurred again. But this time, because he had experienced one break already and was working hard in therapy, he recognized the second break coming. He was aware that his mind was starting to take off, attempting to split from reality. Like the alcoholic learning how his mind tries to trick him into drinking, he became aware of his mind's wanting to take off on its own course.

Fortunately he was dedicated enough that at the onset of the second psychotic break, he was able to understand the similarities between how he began to change (dissociate) the first time and what was occurring the second time.

So what did we do? We had him go back on a low dosage of medication to keep him from experiencing a second episode. Once his mind calmed down and he had a few additional therapy sessions, we took him off his medication.

By using the medication in this manner, we only had to use a minimum amount because he had not developed a strong tolerance for it. It was also easier for him to again stop the medication when he no longer needed it.

A similar approach is recommended by Loren Mosher, M.D., who was as experienced as anyone working with this population. He believed that a sedative would work well in such situations to slow the mind down, after which the client could back off the sedative as soon as possible.

This is a very important point. If antipsychotic medication is used with the belief that it can eventually cure or control the problem, a dependency on the drug (or other drugs) will result. But if it is understood that a drug is only going to be used for a short time to slow the mind down, the focus will be on recovery and a healing solution.

The man with the back problem chose to go back on medication a third time and then quickly go off of it again. But each time he followed this procedure, he was able to learn more about the buildup, and eventually he took conscious control of it, much the same as an alcoholic in recovery.

From my own perspective, this man was a most ideal case. He broke from reality and was diagnosed with paranoid schizophrenia by a seasoned psychiatrist, but he was both intelligent and committed enough to progress rapidly in recovery. As a former engineer, he was extremely analytical and wanted to figure it all out for himself.

He, like Dan Fisher and others who have recovered from psychotic episodes, eventually saw his breakdown as a "breakthrough" and thus a blessing. He had developed some extremely destructive emotional habits. After years of judging himself and the world, he needed to break free of such self-defeating patterns. In addition, off all medication, he was an excellent stay-at-home father and was able to fully concentrate on some part-time work, as well as feel confident in caring for his children. While some medication had helped to temporarily numb him against painful feelings before they created another psychotic episode, he needed to be off medication and fully aware in order to connect past events to those feelings.

Back to Example 1

Our original college student client had a willing attitude but was not nearly as responsive as the man with the back problem. Nevertheless, she did accept what I was trying to teach her enough to return to school after only three sessions. Her parents, the client, and I together decided it would be best for her to stay on medication as she made the adjustment of returning to school, finding a counselor, and beginning the healing process.

At school she entered into therapy with a local therapist and began to more formally address her self-image problems. Fortunately she did not experience a relapse and eventually gradually reduced and then ceased her medication intake.

In this case, even though she was embarrassed when the break took place, a correct understanding and handling of this time in her life resulted in a big step forward in her emotional maturity.

Unfortunately, not all cases are this easy to resolve. But with a proper view of what causes a psychotic break, we would have a lot more successful cases.

Example 3: A More Difficult Case

So far I have presented some fairly simple-to-understand cases. The truth is that many individuals diagnosed with schizophrenia have extremely complicated and diverse delusional systems that have been developed over the course of their lives.

In complicated cases, an extraordinary amount of patience may be required on the part of the professional. Ira Steinman, in his book *Treating the "Untreatable": Healing in the Realms of Madness*,[30] presented several valuable case studies. While some of these cases required him to hospitalize the patient and prescribe medication, his goal was to help these individuals recover from their condition and eventually live medication-free lives.

In Chapter Eight of his book, he presented one of his examples. When Dr. Steinman started with Daphne, she had already been hospitalized more than 35 times and had made several attempts at suicide. After he had worked with her for several months, she finally shared with him that she had been talking with "Mary," who turned out to be a fictitious friend that she had created at the age of three. When Daphne was one-and-a-half years old, her mother gave birth to another daughter. After Daphne's mother switched much of her attention over to the newborn, Daphne became jealous, and by age two-and-a-half, she had developed a strong hatred towards her younger sister. Steinman related that one time, when Daphne was on the front porch with her sister, who was in a baby carriage, "an older girl appeared above Daphne's head, and told her to push the baby carriage off the porch."[31] Steinman related that this older girl was eventually named "Mary" and was interwoven into much of Daphne's delusional system. According to Steinman, Daphne was later molested by her father. While this was happening, "Daphne would go off and play with her friend in the air while her father heaved away on the bed."[32] (Again, this is not the work of a defective brain, but of a creative, protective mind.)

Here is a nearly perfect example in which a delusional system or fictitious person was created from a more normal stressful event (the birth of a sibling), but then later was expanded upon when the child faced more serious forms of trauma (incest). For years, even when Daphne later married and was raising her own family, it often appeared to her husband and children that Daphne was talking to someone as she stared off into space.

When Steinman first noticed her looking beyond him, he asked her what she was staring at. She did not tell him about Mary until later, but revealed that her previous psychiatrists (remember, over 35 hospitalizations) had never asked her that question. It was the questioning, patience with the process, and building of the necessary safety that eventually revealed the identity of Mary, her delusional system, and the emotional pain behind her delusions.

Steinman did have to hospitalize her and prescribe medication at times, in part because she became suicidal when she attempted to give up the security of her fictitious friend and companion. But according to Steinman, "Little by little over the next few months, some of it in the hospital, she relinquished a delusional system that had lasted fifty-five years."[33]

Although healed and recovered, when she is under stress, Daphne may still see and talk to Mary, like the woman who saw bugs or how I went blind in front of an audience. But she now understands why she created Mary and at times needed Mary's support and assistance to maintain her sanity. She can still become fragile at times, like any of us, but she now is in a position to control her own destiny.

ADDRESSING THE THERAPEUTIC PROBLEM— SOME ADDITIONAL CLARITY

Let me go back to my stick figure to help us better understand how the overall therapeutic program or problem should be addressed.

Distorted thoughts
and out-of-control ———————→
behavior

Violated
feelings and
experiences ———→
suppressed out
of awareness

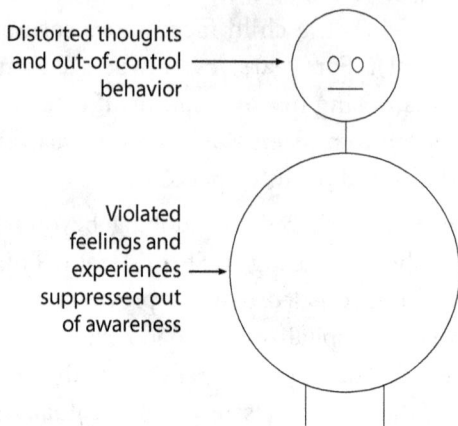

When I approach almost anyone who is seeking help and is hurting for personal or relational reasons, I often use the above diagram as my basic model and approach. At times I will approach the problem by trying to help the person correctly identify his or her painful feelings, or I may start by helping the person with his or her distorted thoughts. Let's again look at a couple of examples, yet always remembering that each person's situation is unique.

OUT-OF-CONTROL THOUGHTS

One of the best examples is the personal testimony of Clifford Beers. In 1900, he was confined to a private mental institution for depression and paranoia. At the height of his paranoia, he did not speak to his family or anyone else for two years. After considerable time had passed, during which he spoke to no one, Beers eventually began to communicate with a very talkative fellow resident. According to Beers:

> A man who during his life had more than once been
> committed to an institution took a very evident interest in

me and persisted in talking to me, often much against my will.... He finally gained my confidence to such a degree that months before I finally began to talk to others I permitted myself to converse frequently with him.[34]

When Beers finally felt comfortable enough, he reported to his friend that the individuals who claimed to be his relatives and came to visit him were not actually his family. When his friend told him that they *were* his relatives, Beers replied, "They look like my relatives, but they're not."[35] His friend then followed with a burst of laughter and said, "Well, if you mean that... you are really the craziest person I have ever met, and I have met several."[36]

This feedback eventually led to a major "moment of clarity." Prior to his brother's next planned visit, Beers sent a letter to him telling him that if he was truly his brother, he must bring that letter, referring to it as his passport. When his brother showed up with the letter and attempted to present it, Beers replied, "There is no need of that. I am convinced."[37] Beers then stated:

> The very instant I caught sight of my letter in the hands of my brother, all was changed. The thousands of false impressions recorded during the seven hundred and ninety-eight days of my depression seemed at once to correct themselves. Untruth became Truth. A large part of what was once my old world was again mine. To me, at last my mind seemed to have found itself, for the gigantic web of false beliefs in which it had been all but hopelessly enmeshed I now immediately recognized as a snare of delusions.[38]

Ultimately, it was a talkative fellow patient (friend)—one who would not leave him alone, who kept joking with him and eventually challenged his delusional state—who began to free Beers from his distorted thinking.

Once our minds begin to distort our reality, any of us—Beers, a married couple, a kid attempting to deny a wrongdoing, a politician, or a person who has been given a diagnosis of schizophrenia—need help finding our way back at times. In addition to the safety and trust that is necessary, it often requires a lot of courage to take an honest look at ourselves and how we have misinterpreted or distorted our reality.

For example, can you imagine the embarrassment that Beers had to face when he finally "woke up," so to speak? And, as I write these words, I am remembering a few times when I was confronted with some of my own distorted truths, and then struggled over whether or not to be honest with others and especially myself.

OVERWHELMING AMOUNT OF EMOTIONAL PAIN

Remember, it is the pain of felt violations that is driving our minds in out-of-control ways. So, obviously, the other basic approach is to address the underlying pain.

The best example that I can give you at this point is to go back to the young lady who suffered from a psychotic break while away at college. Luckily, her mind had not distorted reality to the point that she could not begin to address her pain of not liking herself and feeling inadequate as a person.

Once again, for any of us, not just the so-called schizophrenic, when our minds take off, or we are too angry about a particular situation, or we are distorting our reality or other individuals, we need to be able to slow our minds down to address the underlying pain.

Let me present another example that I have used at times to explain how I approach both the cognitive side and the feeling side of the equation. This example illustrates just how unique each situation can become, and how simply giving a person a diagnosis of schizophrenia and then medicating (actually drugging) the person does not address the core issues properly.

This is the case of a man who had come to believe that he was half man and half woman. He lived in a small town where most individuals knew him and his claim, since he did not hesitate to tell anyone of this condition. He had been diagnosed with schizophrenia by at least two professionals. The case was eventually referred to me.

After a few sessions, he began to tell me about his past. As a young boy, he had been sexually abused by an older stepbrother, and this abuse had gone on for a couple of years while the stepbrother lived in his home. Eventually the stepbrother moved out. Shortly after that, however, a younger cousin came to visit, and my client molested him.

The combination of these experiences eventually overloaded him with the shame of being abused, the guilt of abusing his cousin, and the terror beneath these feelings. Believing that it was wrong for his stepbrother to abuse him, he could not handle the thought that he had committed the same act against his younger cousin.

When he reached the point of possibly experiencing a psychotic break due to an overload of these feelings, his mind came to his rescue and created a solution. He already knew or believed that he was a man. But, if he could believe he was part woman, it would then make it at least "somewhat okay" that he had a sexual encounter with his male cousin. I can't remember if this was his true interpretation, but this distortion of reality was enough to keep his strong destructive feelings in check.

Once he was able to talk about both abusive situations and we understood the meaning behind his belief system, he began to forgive himself. By not feeling judged by me and by forgiving himself, the need to believe he was half man and half woman eventually disappeared.

Following is a stick-figure diagram of his situation. It is best read and understood from the bottom up.

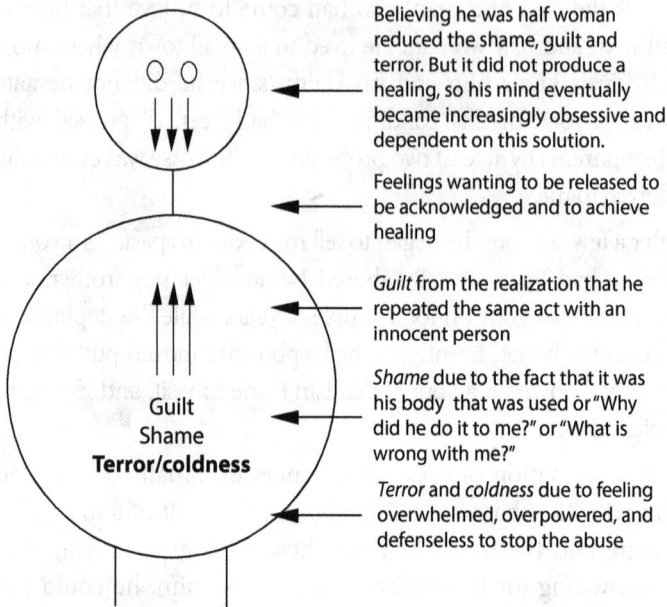

Believing he was half woman reduced the shame, guilt and terror. But it did not produce a healing, so his mind eventually became increasingly obsessive and dependent on this solution.

Feelings wanting to be released to be acknowledged and to achieve healing

Guilt from the realization that he repeated the same act with an innocent person

Shame due to the fact that it was his body that was used or "Why did he do it to me?" or "What is wrong with me?"

Terror and *coldness* due to feeling overwhelmed, overpowered, and defenseless to stop the abuse

Guilt
Shame
Terror/coldness

He and I approached the problem and produced a healing by addressing his distorted thoughts and beliefs about himself, as well as addressing the shame and guilt that he felt.

Once again, to mature properly, each person must eventually address the painful events in his or her life through the healing of those events and by overcoming the distortion of his or her cognitive thoughts. Such a process may need to occur as a result of a hard day's work, from a marital dispute, or from more violating events in the past.

A FINAL EXAMPLE

To be absolutely truthful, I have learned so much more about the so-called condition of schizophrenia in particular and recovery in general from individuals who have successfully lived through the experience. After all, are we not talking about human life experiences rather than physical diseases? If someone was a witness to a terrible or important event, we often want a first-hand account of every detail of their *lived experience*.

One person who taught me a lot was the young girl who hallucinated bugs. According to her, she found it absolutely necessary to use both cognitive and inner healing approaches, as well as some psychotropic medication.

If you remember, her mind created the bugs as a way to distract her from the shame in her life as a result of childhood abuse. When the shame would begin to surface, the bugs would appear, causing her mind to race and thus avoid focusing on the painful feelings that could send her into a deep depression, even to the point of possibly taking her own life.

If you think about it for a moment, we all have our special ways of distracting ourselves from painful feelings, whether it is boredom, the loss of a loved one, or whatever. But if we are trying to avoid a more intense painful moment like the loss of a loved one, we can all probably remember having to work hard to keep our minds off the pain of the event. And, if we try to relax, go to sleep, and so forth, our minds will soon compel us to dwell upon that painful experience. Our minds keep trying to return us to the "scene of the crime," because our sense of self or soul has been wounded and is crying out for a healing, or at least, a resolution of some sort.

A recent incident provides a good example of this. I do most of my writing in fast food coffee shops. For some reason I can concentrate best at such places. While at a coffee shop not long ago, one of the employees came up to me and started talking about her family. When I asked about her husband, she said he had passed away just a few years ago. At that point I saw tears start to well up in her eyes. She then said, "I have to stay busy on the job especially or I will start crying at times," and off she went.

So if each of us must respond in such a way because of more "common" life experiences, how important were the bugs to my client?

It is also important to note that whenever the above client felt any possible shame coming from another person, it would trigger her deeper pain and then the bugs would surface. For example, if I tried to move the therapeutic process along too quickly, she would feel like she was failing me. Such a situation would then trigger the deeper shame of when she was told by her mother that she would always be a failure.

Actually, she felt or believed she was failing me because I had certain expectations that I could move at a particular pace. I did not intentionally mean to trigger her shame, but I certainly had no idea as to what an appropriate pace should be. After all, I had not even come close to experiencing what she had. In fact, as a result of working with severely abused individuals, I now instruct them in the following way. I tell them,

> I do not know what your limits are because I can't jump inside your body and get an accurate reading. So, I need your help. If we are moving too fast or getting into areas that you are not ready for, let me know. We need to work together.

Such instructions almost always calms a person down and this helps to create the necessary safety to move forward. This approach especially helps when trying to prevent the use of psychotropic drugs.

Let's now return to the woman who was hallucinating the bugs. On one hand, the bugs were "necessary" to keep her from hurting herself, but this hallucination was also obviously counterproductive at times. For example, if she was in a grocery store shopping for herself and an impatient person just by chance gave her an angry or shaming look, the bugs would soon appear and she would then need to leave the store without completing her shopping.

So, she needed to approach the problem with the bugs in two main ways, as depicted by the following diagram.

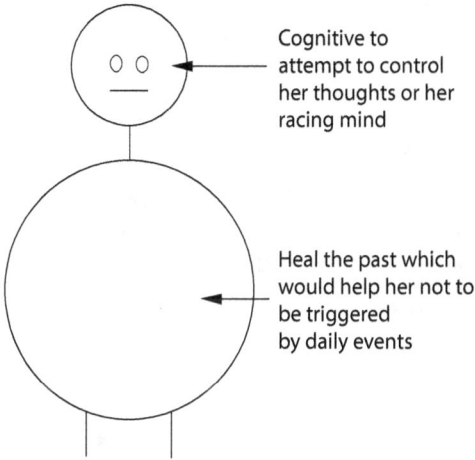

Cognitive to attempt to control her thoughts or her racing mind

Heal the past which would help her not to be triggered by daily events

Let's again go through the different major therapeutic modalities as depicted by the earlier diagram.

DRUG THERAPY

Remember, drugs work by disabling the brain. Thus, if the pain is great enough, or if a person's present external living situation is not conducive or safe enough to do intensive therapeutic work, perhaps a drug may help. The above client did take a sleeping pill once in a while because sleep deprivation was causing her to lose additional control, precipitating more bugs and other problems. But she was also careful not to use the sleeping pills more than a couple of nights in a row because of their addictive potential.

She especially did not want to start on an antipsychotic because she was quite aware from past experience that she would not be able to heal and recover while "drugged up" (her words).

This does not completely eliminate the use of antipsychotics. On the other hand, the use of any mind-altering substances, including alcohol or street drugs, could and usually does eventually inhibit the recovery and healing process.

TWELVE-STEP PROGRAMS

Fortunately, she did not have any major out-of-control behaviors such as food, spending, or drugs. In any case, she was quite determined to survive and heal so she would not have hesitated to be involved in the appropriate twelve-step program if necessary.

COGNITIVE THERAPY

I have been able to follow this case for many years because soon after she started with me, I referred her to a female therapist who is excellent in inner healing work. So, when I approached this ex-client to ask her about the use of cognitive therapy, on one hand she confirmed some of my beliefs. But she also expanded my knowledge in reference to the use of cognitive therapy.

I first asked her if she had done any pure cognitive therapy work that focused just on controlling her thoughts, and if so, did that help? She said she had done this with another therapist before she started with me. This more traditionally trained cognitive therapist actually made the situation worse because this client needed the bugs to help control the shame. In fact, the cognitive-orientated therapist had tried, but she had also insisted on the use of antipsychotic medications to help handle the hallucinations. So, in a sense, this client's subconscious was saying, "I need the bugs to survive until I sufficiently heal from my past."

On the other hand, and especially when she finally started with a therapist who focused more on the healing of her past violations, this client on her own brought a lot of cognitive-orientated help into her life. When the bugs would appear, she would start questioning them or challenging herself. She would say to herself, "How can they be real if there are so many?" or "Why do they not seem to be afraid of me?" or "Why do others not seem to be afraid of them or notice them?"

So, in one sense, through the creation of the bugs, she was able to keep her shame (as well as her loneliness and hurt) under control. But at the same time, by challenging the awareness of the bugs, it allowed her to start functioning at a higher level in her external world.

INNER HEALING

Thus, a cognitive or rational-oriented approach certainly helped her somewhat by challenging the validity of the hallucinations. But she still needed to be healed of the past violations in her life. In other words, since she had been violated and disaffirmed by people she trusted (or needed to trust), she needed to be reaffirmed by people she trusted, mainly in the safety provided by a skilled therapist.

By focusing on her deeper pain at times, letting it up, verbalizing it, and fully re-experiencing the corresponding feelings, and then being affirmed by her therapist (and group members), a healing began to take place. As an inner healing began to develop, she became stronger and, in a sense, the bugs were not needed as much.

Furthermore, as she gradually learned to trust the therapist, when the bugs would appear, she had an additional source of *truth* or form of cognitive therapy to rely upon. At times, she would email her therapist, as well as her trusted group members, to obtain additional support and feedback if needed. Her therapist allowed this extra help because she knew the client needed it, but she also trusted that the client would not abuse this extra service. Actually, just knowing that she could email her therapist gave her the additional safety she needed to attempt to move forward on her own.

SUMMARY OF THIS CASE

To be honest with you, this was a very difficult case based mainly on the severity of the abuse and the length of time she was subjected to the abuse. The abuse took place from early childhood into her 20s. But it is from such extremely severe and successful cases that we can often learn the most.

For some individuals, cognitive therapy may be sufficient. Richard Beers may be a prime example. Once someone he trusted (fellow patient) untwisted his mind, he then had a place of truth to work from. But with the lady in this example, the shame (and other negative feelings) was so great, that without an inner healing, cognitive therapy would not have worked. In fact, only marginal gains would have been realized which, unfortunately, may have satisfied the cognitive-orientated therapist, as well as researchers focusing on a cognitive approach.

What may then be missing is for cognitive and inner healing programs to work together. The above client, who is now an excellent therapist, said she would approach a similar situation by seeing a client twice a week. During one session, she would work on the deep pain. During the other session, she would work from the cognitive side. And of course, if the person was doing well from a cognitive perspective, she could spend more time on the inner healing side. Or, if an external issue surfaced, setting off or triggering the person's shame, the cognitive side could be stressed with extra focus.

And, as a last resort, if a drug was needed, then it could be applied hopefully on a short-term basis. But the ultimate goal would be to work back and forth from the cognitive to the inner healing to help the person toward a full recovery.

In closing, because each situation is different, and the hurting person will have unique needs, the helper must be prepared to adjust to that person's specific situation and needs, rather than have the person adjust to the therapist's needs or his or her personal brand of therapy.

Additional Resources

FORTUNATELY, A GROWING NUMBER of resources are available that can help people diagnosed with schizophrenia. Unfortunately, at this point most of these resources are educational in nature. I say unfortunately because what is needed more than anything is more professionals who are willing to help suffering individuals from a healing and recovery perspective, not a "disease" perspective.

But on the plus side, the growing number of educational resources is creating a path for the development of more healing and recovery-oriented helpers.

FIRST CHOICE:
YOUTUBE TESTIMONIES AND WRITTEN MATERIAL BY SURVIVORS

Check out the following materials by Drs. Dan Fisher and Pat Deegan. Like Dan Fisher, Pat Deegan was also diagnosed with schizophrenia, recovered, went back to school to obtain her doctorate, and then dedicated her life to helping others successfully recover.

Dan Fisher   "The Open Paradigm Project"
                (YouTube video),
                https:/www.youtube.com/
                watch?v=VcJivL1ksIU

A New Vision of Recovery (booklet), www.Power2u.org

Pat Deegan "Recovery From Mental Disorders, A Lecture by Patricia Deegan" (YouTube video), https://www.youtube.com/watch?v=jhK-7DkWaKE

I Don't Think It Was My Treatment Plan That Made Me Well (booklet), http://store.patdeegan.com/collections/manuscripts

SECOND CHOICE:
READ *FROM BREAKDOWN TO BREAKTHROUGH WORKBOOK*

The title of my workbook indirectly came from survivors such as Dan Fisher and Pat Deegan, who created their own healing and recovery programs after receiving a diagnosis of schizophrenia. Once these individuals decided to address their personal issues, they soon realized that their "breakdown" was a blessing in disguise because it had created the path to a "breakthrough" in their lives.

This is an educational workbook that all parties, including the suffering person and his or her helpers, can equally learn from as they participate together in the exercises. In fact, it is recommended that a separate workbook be purchased for each participant.

Rather than immediately starting to do the work outlined in the workbook, I suggest that it first be read through in order to get a better idea of what needs to take place in a healing and recovery program. The actual study and completion of the workbook *should be postponed* until the proper therapist and support team are assembled.

THIRD CHOICE:
WRAP PROGRAM

As a suffering person, a good place to start may be to look into Mary Ellen Copeland's material, including her WRAP program (http://mentalhealthrecovery.com). By the way, she is also a person in recovery (from depression) who has gone on to build programs to help others.

FOURTH CHOICE:
SUPPORTIVE WEBSITES

The following websites represent organizations that adhere to the basic principles in this book and contain a lot of wonderful educational material, including additional books and resources. It will be well worth the time of interested parties to check out these sites.

The International Society for Psychological and Social Approaches to Psychosis (ISPS) is an international organization promoting psychotherapy and psychological treatments for persons with psychosis (including persons diagnosed with schizophrenia). ISPS is committed to advancing education, training, and knowledge of mental health professionals in the treatment and prevention of psychotic mental disorders. This organization seeks to achieve the best possible outcomes for service user/ survivors by engaging in meaningful partnership with health professionals, service user/survivors, families, and careers. (*www.isps.org*)

Center for the Study of Empathic Therapy, Education & Living. This center is devoted to examining the false theories and dangerous practices of biological psychiatry and to replacing them with more humane and caring approaches. (www.empathictherapy.org)

The International Society for Ethical Psychology and Psychiatry (ISEPP) is a nonprofit organization of mental health professionals, researchers, lawyers, parents, families, teachers, and others who study and promote safe, humane, life-enhancing approaches to help people who are diagnosed with mental disorders. (*www.psychIntegrity.org*)

National Empowerment Center. The organization's mission is to "Carry a message of recovery, empowerment, hope, and healing to people with lived experience with mental health issues, trauma, and extreme states." (*www.power2u.org*)

MindFreedom International. MindFreedom is a nonprofit organization that unites over 100 sponsor and affiliate grassroots groups with thousands of individual members to win human rights and alternatives for people labeled with psychiatric disabilities. (*www.mindfreedom.org*).

International Hearing Voices Network (Intervoice) is an international community dedicated to sharing information about hearing voices, including an online forum, stories, groups, news, and publications. (*www.intervoiceonline.org*)

Hearing Voices Network is committed to helping people who hear voices. HVN's reputation is growing as the limitations of a solely medical approach to voices become better known. Psychiatry refers to hearing voices as "auditory hallucinations," but research shows that there are many explanations for hearing voices. Many people begin to hear voices as a result of extreme stress or trauma. (*www.hearing-voices.org*)

The Copeland Center for Wellness and Recovery transforms lives by promoting wellness, recovery, and peer support through training, technical assistance, and advocacy. The organization produces a wealth of information, including research, newsletters, and books. (www.copelandcenter.com)

Schizophreniarecovery.net. A website with lots of excellent material on the psychotherapy of schizophrenia. The directors of this website share their experience in the effective treatment of schizophrenia which over the past 50 years has illustrated that there is hope for even the most severely regressed person with schizophrenia. The information center's mission is to expose those diagnosed with schizophrenia who are considered to be treatment-resistant, to an atmosphere of hope and a treatment model that considers the healthy parts of the individual as the important focus. (www.schizophreniarecovery.net)

Beyond Meds: Monica Cassani (www.beyondmeds.com) has experienced the system from both sides—as a social worker and as a person whose life was severely ruptured by psychiatric drugs. She writes critically about the system, as well as about holistic pathways of healing without medication. You can read her biography at www. madinamerica.com /2013/05/before-during-after-psychdrugs.)

Working to Recovery. An organization run by Ron Coleman and his wife Karen that helps individuals recover from emotional trauma. Ron and Karen also present workshops for therapists. (www.workingtorecovery.co.uk)

PsychRights. The Law Project for Psychiatric Rights (PsychRights) is a non-profit public interest law firm whose mission is to mount a strategic legal campaign against forced psychiatric drugging and electroshock in the United States. This site contains many excellent articles and other useful information. (*www.psychrights.org*)

The International Network Toward Alternatives and Recovery (INTAR) gathers prominent survivors, professionals, family members, and advocates from around the world to work together for new clinical and social practices in response to emotional distress and what is often labeled as psychosis. Based on leading-edge research and successful innovations, INTAR believes the prevailing biomedical overreliance on diagnoses, hospitals, and medications has failed to respect the dignity and autonomy of the person in crisis, and that full recovery must be at the center of ethical care. (*www.intar.org*)

Coming Off Psychiatric Drugs. This website aims to give individuals up-to-date information about psychiatric medication, how it functions, and the withdrawal process. It is put together by people who have been prescribed medication and withdrawn from it, and by clinicians who have been involved in supporting this process. You can download the booklet Harm Reduction Guide at this site. (*www.comingoff.com*)

Mad In America. The website serves as a resource and a community for those interested in rethinking psychiatric care in the United States and abroad. It provides readers with news, personal stories, access to source documents, and the informed writings of bloggers that will further this enterprise. (*www.madinamerica.com*)

National Association for Rights Protection and Advocacy. NARPA's mission is to promote policies and pursue strategies that allow individuals with psychiatric diagnoses to make their own choices regarding treatment. The association educates and mentors those individuals to enable them to exercise their legal and human rights, with a goal of abolition of all forced treatment. (www.narpa.org)

FIFTH CHOICE:
ADDITIONAL READING MATERIAL

Fight to Be: A Psychologist's Experience from Both Sides of the Locked Door by survivor Ron Bassman (autobiography). (Albany, NY: Tantamount Press, 2007)

Alternatives Beyond Psychiatry edited by Peter Stastny and Peter Lehmann. A book full of information from professionals and survivors of a diagnosis of schizophrenia and psychosis. (Berlin: Peter Lehmann, 2007)

Healing Runaway Minds by Ty C. Colbert. My book goes into much more detail than this brief book, regarding the true origin of such conditions as schizophrenia, the role of feelings, and the healing and recovery process. (Orange, CA: Kevco, 2016)

Recovery: An Alien Concept? by Ron Coleman, another psychiatric survivor who is currently helping others to recover. (P&P Books, 2011)

Treating The "Untreatable" by Ira Steinman. Dr. Steinman has worked with people diagnosed with schizophrenia for 45 years. In this book he shares many stories of recovery. (London: Karnac Books, 2009)

Catch Them Before They Fall by Christopher Bollas. Dr. Bollas suggests that the "unconscious purpose of a breakdown is to present the self to the other for a transformative understanding," or in essence, as I have claimed, a cry for help. He suggests and presents cases studies of intervention right before a major psychotic break takes place. (New York: Routledge, 2013.)

Cognitive-Behavioral Therapy of Schizophrenia by David G. Kingdom and Douglas Turkington. This book lays out the basic foundation for a cognitive approach to schizophrenia or psychosis. (New York: The Guilford Press, 1994)

The International Society for Psychological and Social Approaches to Psychosis material. Their website contains several books on the subject of the psychotherapy of schizophrenia or psychosis (*www.isps.org*).

Breakdown to Breakthrough by Ty C. Colbert. A healing and recovery workbook for the suffering individuals, professionals and for helpers concerned about individuals diagnosed with "schizophrenia."

SIXTH CHOICE:
MINIMIZING OR ELIMINATING THE USE OF
PSYCHOTROPIC MEDICATIONS

As I have already mentioned, these drugs work by disabling the brain; they do not fix some defect. Therefore, once a proper healing, recovery, and support system is in place, many survivors have been able to minimize or eliminate the use of these substances with caution and professional help. The following is a list of reference materials for this topic.

Breggin, P. *Psychiatric Drug Withdrawal: A Guide for Prescribers, Therapists, Patients and Their Families.* New York: Singer, 2013.

Breggin, P., and D. Cohen. *Your Drug May Be Your Problem: How and Why to Stop Taking Psychiatric Medications.* Cambridge, MA: Da Capo Press, 2007.

Hall, W. *Harm Reduction Guide to Coming Off Psychiatric Drugs,* 2nd Ed. Northampton, MA: The Icarus Project & the Freedom Center, June 2012. See http://www.freedom-center.org/freedom-center-icarus-project-publish-coming-psychiatric-drugs-guide.

Lehmann, P. (Ed.). *Coming off Psychiatric Drugs.* Eugene OR: Peter Lehmann Publishing, 1998. See http://www.peter-lehmann-publishing.com/withdraw/prefaces.htm.

Cassani, M. "Psychiatric Drug Withdrawal and Protracted Withdrawal Syndrome Round-Up." Posted December 4, 2012, in *Beyond Meds: Alternatives to Psychiatry.* http://beyondmeds.com/2012/12/04/psychiatric-drug-withdrawal.

Charlton, B. G. *Why are doctors still prescribing neuroleptics?* Retrieved October 1, 2014, from http://www.hedweb.com/bgcharlton/neuroleptics.

Copeland, M. E. "Recipe for Recovery: A Guide to Reducing or Eliminating Psychiatric Medications." http://www.wrapandrecoverybooks.com/recovery-resources/articles.php?id=75.

Deegan, P. (9/17/14). *Reclaiming your power during medication appointments with your psychiatrist.* National Empowerment Center. http://power2u.org/articles/selfhelp/reclaim.html.

Quitting Psychiatric Drugs Info Compiled by MindFreedom. http://www.mindfreedom.org/kb/psychiatric-drugs/quitting.

Unger, R. "Helping Reduce Medications." *Recovery from "Schizophrenia" and Other "Psychotic Disorders.* http://recoveryfromschizophrenia.org/therapists-guide-to-reducing-medications.

A FEW CLOSING WORDS

Hopefully this small book will help those individuals suffering from the so-called condition of schizophrenia to begin a proper healing and recovery program. Perhaps the most important point to remember is that no one makes it through life without emotionally struggling at times. Such moments can include a diagnosis of a mental illness, a divorce, a bankruptcy, the death of a loved one, and so on. Remember, a mental illness diagnosis is just an emotional stage in life, possibly a difficult one, but one a person can eventually overcome. When these emotional stages are conquered properly, individuals come out happier, stronger, and more in control of their lives. Such a positive result has taken place in the lives of thousands of individuals who were once given a diagnosis of schizophrenia. Fortunately for them, it was not an everlasting diagnosis, but just a temporary moment in time.

References

1. S. E. Hyman and E. J. Nestler, "Initiation and Adaptation: A Paradigm for Understanding Psychotropic Drug Action," *American Journal of Psychiatry*, Vol. 153, No. 2 (February 1996), pp. 151–162.

2. J. O. Johannessen, email (November 16, 2915), jan.olav.johannessen@sus.no.

3. P. Thamas, *Pinball Wizards and the Doomed Project of Psychiatric Disorders*, retrieved December 12, 2015, from https://www.madinamerica.com/2013/02/pinball-wizards-and-the-doomed-project-of-psychiatric-diagnosis.

4. Ibid.

5. R. Whitaker, *Anatomy of an Epidemic* (New York: Crown Publishers, 2010), p. 110.

6. P. Breggin, *Brain-Disabling Treatments in Psychiatry* (New York: St. Martin's Press, 2008), p. 374.

7. A. Jablensky, "Multicultural Studies and the Nature of Schizophrenia: A Review," *Journal of the Royal Society of Medicine*, Vol. 80 (1987), pp. 162–67.

8. R. Whitaker, *Mad in America* (Cambridge, MA: Perseus Publishing, 2002), p. 231.

9. P. Williams, *Rethinking Madness* (San Rafael, CA: Sky's Edge Publishing, 2012).

10. D. Fisher, *A New Vision of Recovery* (Lawrence, MA: National Empowerment Center, 2007), p.2.

11. Ibid., p. 17.

12. G. A. Hornstein, *To Redeem One Person Is to Redeem the World* (New York: Other Press, 2000), p. 123.

13. Ibid.

14. J. Chambers, *The Conscious Mind: In Search of a Fundamental Theory* (New York: Oxford University Press, 1996), p. xi.

15. Ibid., p. xii.

16. N. S. Sutherland (Ed.), *The International Dictionary of Psychology* (New York: Continuum, 1989).

17. J. Rosen, *Direct Analysis: Selected Papers* (New York: Grune & Stratton, 1953), p. 6.

18. P. Duke and H. Gloria, *A Brilliant Madness* (New York: Bantam, 1992), p. 9.

19. E. Bleuler, *Dementia Praecox or the Group of Schizophrenias* (1911), J. Zinkin, Trans. (New York: International University Press, 1950), p. 8.

20. A. Moskowitz, "Pierre Janet's Influence on Bleuler's Concept of Schizophrenia," paper presented at the First Symposium of the Pierre Janet Gesellschaft, Freiburg, Germany (June 3–4, 2005), retrieved October 24, 2014, from http://search.yahoo.com/

21. B. Karon, "The Tragedy of Schizophrenia," *The General Psychologist*, Vol. 32, No. 1 (1999), p. 14.

22. Ibid.

23. P. R. Breggin, *Brain Disabling Treatments in Psychiatry* (New York: Springer, 1997).

24. G. Jackson, *Drug-Induced Dementia* (Bloomington, IN: Author House, 2009).

25. http://www.nimh.nih.gov/health/topics/schizophrenia/index.shtml.

26. J. Seikkula, J. Aaltonen, B. Alakare, K. Haarakangas, J. Keränen, & K. Lehtinen, "Five-Year Experience of First-Episode Nonaffective Psychosis in Open-Dialogue Approach: Treatment Principles, Follow-Up Outcomes, and Two Case Studies," *Psychotherapy Research*, Vol. 16, No. 2 (March 2006), pp. 214–228.

27. "Finland Open Dialogue," retrieved October 10, 2012, from http://www.mindfreedom.org/kb/mental-health-alternatives/finland-open-dialogue.

28. Dialogic Practice, retrieved October 10, 2012, from http://www.dialogicpractice.net/.

29. Psychiatric Drugs Are Being Prescribed to Infants, retrieved December 3, 2015, from http://www.nsaneforums.com/topic/257939-psychiatric-drugs-are-being-prescribed-to-infants.

30. I. Steinman, *Treating the "Untreatable"* (London: Karnac Books, 2009).

31. Ibid., p. 56.

32. Ibid.

33. Ibid., p. 59.

34. C. W. Beers, *A Mind That Found Itself* (Pittsburgh, PA: University of Pittsburgh Press, 1981), p. 11.

35. Ibid.

36. Ibid.

37. Ibid., p. 45.

38. Ibid.

www.ingramcontent.com/pod-product-compliance
Lightning Source LLC
Chambersburg PA
CBHW050550280326
41933CB00011B/1791